BENEATH THE SURFACE

AN ANTHOLOGY OF WRITING FROM LAKE MACQUARIE

Editors

KJ Mair, Pam Garfoot,

Alison Ferguson, Linda Visman

First published in Australia in 2020 by Lake Macquarie Branch, Fellowship of Australian Writers NSW
www.lakemacfaw2.wordpress.com

Beneath the Surface: An anthology of writing from Lake Macquarie
ISBN-13-978-1-876409-63-0 (paperback)
ISBN-13-978-1-876409-49-4 (e-book)

Cover design by Scott Mair
Illustrations by Pam Garfoot

Contents

Foreword

Writing can be a solitary and uncertain activity. That's why associations like the Fellowship of Australian Writers (FAW) are so important. They bring experienced and novice writers together, encouraging mentorships, collaboration, feedback, and submissions. The Lake Macquarie FAW holds monthly meetings in which they encourage one another to try new things and expand writing skills in a safe, inclusive workshop atmosphere. I've been lucky enough to have been invited several times as a guest presenter, and also as a judge for the locally run Alice Sinclair competition. Whenever I've attended one of their sessions, I have been consistently impressed with the calibre of the work produced, and the warm camaraderie and support throughout the group. *Beneath the Surface* is a testimony to that spirit and presents some of the best, most powerful work being produced by the Lake Macquarie FAW.

There are 28 pieces in *Beneath the Surface,* spanning multiple genres including memoir, fiction, historical fiction, horror, ghost stories, and poetry. The work often utilises local settings, from the shores of Wangi Wangi to Newcastle pubs. Without exception, the writers make use of their experiences to create rich verisimilitude in the work. The pieces span a broad spectrum of personal and imagined scenarios exploring themes around lost love, brave shenanigans, life lessons and sudden epiphanies. There are a number of stories that trace pivotal moments in personal and more general history, such as a child's experience of the 1989 Newcastle Earthquake against BHP Steelworks, a holiday trip upriver into the Borneo interior, swimming with sharks on Ningaloo Reef, the life-changing transition to retirement, a cousin who married Agatha Christie's ex-husband after a newsworthy affair, and an uncle who fought the Japanese in WWII on the Kokoda Track. These pieces are well-researched, combining fact with an engaging narrative thread that draws the reader in. There is a modern rendition of Romeo and Juliet, monsters both human and otherworldly, and plenty of parental anxiety. There are poems about the power of friendship, hunting herons, ageing, the beauty of the natural world — a common thread through these works, the destructive nature of war, and the mysterious inner life of the family cat.

Editors Kristen Mair, Pam Garfoot, Alison Ferguson, and Linda Visman have done an excellent job selecting a balanced range of pieces, keeping the order beautifully varied, and ensuring that the work fits the "beneath the surface" theme. Many of the pieces included are award winners and/or previously published, and all of them are easy to read, engaging, and well-written. *Beneath the Surface* is beautifully presented, with pen and ink illustrations throughout by the multi-talented Pam Garfoot. The book will appeal to readers of many different genres and tastes, and can be read slowly, in small moments that transform the everyday into something a little richer, or read quickly in one intense sitting. Either way, *Beneath the Surface* is a delight.

Magdalena Ball

(December, 2019)

Magdalena Ball is a novelist, poet, reviewer, interviewer, and the editor of *Compulsive Reader*. She has been widely published in literary journals, anthologies, and is the author of several books of poetry and fiction.

Introduction

Since 2000 the Lake Macquarie Branch of the Fellowship of Australian Writers has been helping local writers develop their writing skills. Through its critique groups it has helped them to improve their writing. Most importantly, the group offers comradeship and support to its members.

When an anthology was suggested members of the group were immediately enthusiastic, though it took another two years before the project got off the ground. Early in 2019 four members took on the task, forming an editorial committee and planning the preparation of the anthology from the initial concept through to its publication and promotion. The committee decided on an intriguing theme, 'Beneath the surface', and encouraged members to get writing. It was exciting to see writers embrace the theme, in all sorts of unexpected ways, and gradually polish their work. The result is this delightful and engaging volume, of which the group can feel very proud.

Works in this anthology represent some of the diversity of genres that the group encourages: poems, short stories, travel stories, and memoir. We thank our writers warmly — for without them this anthology could not have been produced. We also thank Scott Mair for his beautiful cover artwork which so perfectly captures the vision of the theme, and Pam Garfoot for her evocative illustrations. In addition, we are enormously grateful to Magdalena Ball for providing the Foreword and to our reviewers — Jan Dean, Jaye Ford, and Ryan O'Neill — for their support.

Every writer in the anthology, from those new to writing to those who have already published works and received commendations, has offered their very best work. We invite you to take a dive under the surface and immerse yourselves in *Beneath the surface: an anthology of writing from Lake Macquarie.*

KJ Mair, Pam Garfoot,
Alison Ferguson, Linda Visman
Editors

The Dragon of BHP

KJ Mair

Dragons are real. My daddy works with one.

He always ends the day smelling of smoke and brings home a smile that stands out against the soot covering his face. His shoes are usually heavy with dirt, and Mum yells at him a lot for making a mess. Sometimes he has burns up and down his arms and once he had a blister the size of a marble.

I worry about the dragon. In every story I've read, they are angry, and scary. Only a knight could defeat them and save the princess. Dad is like a knight in some ways. I saw him once wearing his armour.

I had snuck away from Mum when we came to bring Dad lunch. I had to squeeze between huge metal doors and through the gloom I spotted my dad. He had big heavy blue overalls on and gloves so thick they could survive Mum's curry without getting hot. But it was the helmet that caught my attention. It looked like it was from medieval times, but had a clear face-guard, so was even cooler. In his hands he held a long pronged fork thing. It was like a sword, but not really. Behind him, the fire hissed and was so hot it felt like sunburn.

But my dad isn't a knight. He's just my dad. When I tell my worries to him, he smiles and musses up my hair with a calloused hand.

"See this?" He pats a badge pinned to his shirt. It's a bird with red feathers down its front and up to its head. "This is the King Parrot, and whenever I wear this, that old dragon has to listen to me and do what I say."

I touch it with care.

"So you wear this every time you go to work?"

"Every time."

I look him dead in the eyes. "You promise?"

"I promise, princess."

~

After dinner, I crouch next to the banister and listen to my parents.

"The guy next to me had his finger lopped off."

I shudder at that, imagining the finger like a disconnected worm, wriggling in its own red pool. I imagine it as Dad's finger and I feel sick.

"What?"

"It was just sitting there, on the shears. The foreman made everyone come and have a look. I think he just wanted to scare the piss out of us." Dad sighs and rubs his face. "I don't think I'll ever forget it."

"Good."

Mum's back is turned and she's scrubbing the pan like she's mad at it.

"What do you mean by that?" Everything becomes very still.

Mum's shoulders drop and the pan falls to the bottom of the sink with a soft *thunk*.

"Have you ever thought about doing something else? Anything else?"

"Jess, what else is there? The steelworks is everything in Newcastle," states Dad.

"I just worry you're putting patches on patches. At some point there's going to be nothing left to patch."

Dad goes to Mum and embraces her from behind. Dad's hugs are the best.

"I think this bloke ditching his digit is a good thing. Think about it, management doesn't want the bad press and losing good men to injuries is no good at all. They have to be putting better work safety stuff in place."

"You think they will?" Mum asks.

"Yeah, I'll be safe as houses."

Mum's quiet for a moment. And then, "Didn't one of your guys die last month? How much has changed since then?"

Dad lets go and doesn't answer her. Mum goes back to the dishes.

For the first time, I don't believe Dad. But I have a plan.

I creep upstairs avoiding the squeaky floorboards. I don't go to my bedroom. Instead I go to my parent's bedroom. Balancing with one foot on the bed and hanging onto the closet door, I'm able to get my dad's work shirt from the coat hanger.

Pinned on the left lapel is the King Parrot badge. The red eyes seem to glare at me as I sneak it into my pocket.

Dad promised he wouldn't go to work without it.

And Dad always keeps his promises.

~

Mum and I are walking in town. My hands sweat, and Mum keeps losing her grip on my fingers.

When I'd gotten up this morning, Dad was gone. His work shirt was missing from the closet and his big heavy boots weren't next to the front door. The only thing not missing is the badge that sits heavy in my pocket.

What will happen now?

As Mum is buying bread it suddenly goes quiet, like the world is holding its breath. Then a crackle. It's the sound of ripping and breaking.

The ground ripples. It's like we are on a sheet that Mum shakes and flings out before she lays it down on the bed.

Mum holds me tight against her chest. I feel the hammering of her heart. It's like it's shaking the ground beneath us. I want her to stop it. I want *it* to stop.

"Oh, Lord, what's happening?" Mum cries.

Between the gap of Mum's pearls and her frilly frock, I see big balls of black smoke. Suddenly, I know what it is ...

The dragon.

The dragon is mad and it's all my fault.

"I'm sorry." I say it again and again, but I don't think anyone hears me.

Around us people are screaming, crying. One even shouts, "Earthquake!"

But I know the truth.

~

It's dark and the sirens are still wailing when I see my dad again. His eyes are wide and he belts towards us.

I leap into his arms and dig in tight. Holding out the badge, I blubber how sorry I am.

He closes my hand around it. "I don't need it anymore, princess."

He looks at Mum over my shoulder. They share a lovey-dovey look.

"I've decided. I won't be seeing that dragon again."

---

*This story was awarded Second Prize in the *Newcastle Herald* Short Story Competition in 2019.

The Sand Patch

Tony Lang

I awake, gasping, sweating, shaking, terrified. I'd been screaming. Janet shakes me awake. It's the eyes again: the red eyes. Evil eyes. I know it wants me, for I saw it. It's calling me to it. Janet thinks it's just some form of PTSD from my time in the army and later, police. I've never told her the real story.

As usual, I get out of bed. Janet has gone back to sleep — I can hear her soft, gentle breathing. How I envy her! I know that I'll have to go through the whole thing again; write it down, a sort of catharsis, the only way I get some peace that may last for a few nights. Here I am now, in my study, at my computer, typing ...

It happened the Christmas before last, here at Wangi Wangi. We had lots of visitors that year, family and friends and even friends of their friends. Some had to stay at the caravan park.

Wangi was a great spot, right on the shores of Lake Macquarie — but I wanted to leave — I *had to* leave, before it — that *thing*, got me. Janet airily dismissed my pleas to go to Wagga to live. It was hundreds of kilometres away. I thought I'd be safe there. I didn't think it could get me there — or could it? At the very thought, a shudder racked my body. Fear-induced sweat blinded me.

How well I remember that Christmas! It was so summery. The ladies did wonders in the kitchen; the atmosphere was wonderful. We all went to church on Christmas morning and filled a couple of pews. Our Christmas dinner that night — what hilarity! I wished it could have lasted forever.

Next day, Boxing Day, we all decided to do different things. Johnny Harris, a friend of one of the friends who came from Queensland, wanted to do some snorkelling. The girls of course all wanted to check out the post-Christmas sales at Glendale while our lot had booked a day up at the vineyards. That left just Tonkie, Jock and me.

Tonkie, being a cat, found the coolest place in the house for a snooze, so after lunch I decided to take Jock the border collie for his usual walk by the lake shore. It was a great walk around the rocks. As we walked, I saw the usual sights I love. In the shallow water small fish darted in and out of the seaweed, and crabs hid among the rocks. Pretty shells sheltered here and there. I saw a brief flash of silver, as a tiny fish suddenly changed direction. Further along, we climbed a short, steep path about five metres above the water. We always did that.

As Jock sniffed the base of each and every tree, I gazed out across the calm lake, lost in my own thoughts. They were cut short by a loud *plop*. Even without looking, I knew a large fish had jumped clear of the water. It was a familiar sound. My eyes swivelled to the place. Below, several metres from the shore, I saw a large sand patch. I should have been able to see the fish disappearing into the sea grass, for the view of the water from the hill was especially clear. I looked, but the fish had vanished.

I wondered what was puzzling me — and then it dawned. I'd walked along the path many times but had never noticed the sand patch before. There was something else as well … its shape. It was about fifteen metres long and roughly the shape of a fish. At the end, the 'tail' flared, while the other end was rounded, like a fish's head. A couple of large shells were situated roughly where eyes would have been. The torso was long and astoundingly fishlike.

My puzzlement turned to bewilderment. It wasn't natural, I told myself. As I watched I saw a fish approach the sand patch and begin to pass along. That's when my fear began. Half-way along, the fish commenced a frenzied movement, as if in an invisible trap. Before my horrified gaze it was pulled down to the sand patch and 'absorbed' — the only way I can describe it — and was gone.

Suddenly the 'shells' opened, and there were its eyes — piercing red, remorseless, boring into my very soul. I clutched the side of the tree beside me. Terror rose, gorging my throat. Transfixed, almost unable to breathe, I watched the sand patch begin to move slowly over the seaweed.

All the while I was aware of its eyes. This *thing* from some other world watched me, devouring my sanity — but wanting more ... wanting me — *all* of me. I had seen what I wasn't meant to see. I knew it would never let me go until it had me. I was helpless.

Who would believe such a story?

As it drifted away the monster sent me one last, dreadful message. Like a merry-go-round it circles endlessly in my head:

Come to the sand patch, the sand patch. Come down to the sand patch ...

Now I know why on Boxing Day that year Johnny Harris, the snorkeller, vanished.

Hunters

Linda Visman

In still shallows
by casuarina shore,
two slender hunters stalk
in slow motion;
one grey, one white,
both skilled in the hunt,
long, sharp weapons ready.

The heron hunts further along,
inshore from the egret
whose longer neck and stilt legs
allow it to harvest deeper waters
while the smaller bird
reaps the benefit
of shoreward-frightened prey.

The slow stalk, sudden pause
the wait, anticipation –
the sudden lunge
and flash of pointed beak,
bring to mind a photo once seen –
another hunter, of a darker hue
and an older time.

Lithe, slender body and limbs
are poised and ready,
shaggy-shaded eyes alert,
searching deeper waters;
arm and spear, lengthened
by Dreamtime technology,
unwavering, aching to lunge
with deadly speed.

The heron's thrust is fruitless,
though silver scales gleam
in the egret's beak.

And what of that other hunter?
The photograph doesn't show
if his three-pronged spear
found the prey it sought.
Instead the camera holds him
suspended in place and time
— forever the hunter.

The Bush Walk

Elizabeth Hunt

Four pairs of eyes are on me.

"C'mon Mum. You can do it. It's easy."

Easy? It *is* for thirteen-year-old boys. Damn hard for this forty-year-old indoor type.

Why did I agree to come? I should have feigned illness or thought of some other excuse. Then another parent would have had to step in. But they all gave feasible reasons, and indeed better ones than I could, for not taking these four boys on a day's outing.

"It will just be a bush walk on flat ground," they told me. "Nothing strenuous."

No one mentioned the river and the method of crossing it.

Once the boys saw the rope hanging from the tree, they rushed over to it. Then took turns to swing across to the opposite bank in Tarzan-like fashion.

So, here I am alone on one side of the river and they on the other.

I know I have to do it. Somehow I must make myself move. Terror has grounded me and paralysed my limbs, but not my heart, which is pounding so hard I think it will erupt from my chest.

"Just grab the rope and push off," calls Graham, one of my son's friends.

Once again, I look down at the swirling waters of what is really only a creek, but is as formidable as the Pacific Ocean to me at this moment.

"Take a run at it first," suggests my son, Jim.

Now I really must summon up all my courage and physical strength, not only to have a go, but to succeed. You *can* do it, I try to convince myself. For your son's sake, it's vital. Calm yourself, take big breaths.

I walk away from the bank. Then crouch for my take-off. Suddenly I am sprinting. I find the rope, clasp it firmly in my hands, and push off from the tree. I am sailing through the air. I dare not look down. It's too much. My heart is in my throat and I wonder how much longer it will allow me to breathe.

Four boys are cheering me on as though I'm in a great race. I feel a bump. It's not a splash, so I must have touched terra firma. I am overwhelmed with relief and pride. Success, how sweet you are.

The rope seems to have wrapped itself around me. Now hands are pulling it away. The boys are patting me in congratulation.

~

"Are you all right? You haven't broken anything have you?"

Kneeling beside me, looking stricken with worry, is my husband.

"How could I have injured myself, in these bedclothes?"

"You must have had a wild dream."

"Yes," I sigh. "Very wild."

He helps me up. All that's damaged is my pride.

"I'm amazed you were able to sleep in, with all the racket Jim and his mates have been making playing cricket."

Brian watches me closely as I pull my dressing gown on.

"Well, I'll head off to the office now if you're certain you're okay."

I assure him I am, and anyway can rest, as I'm off work today. He shakes his head and gives me a cheeky grin.

"The not working bit's true, but I doubt you'll be resting. Remember this is the day you're taking Jim and his friends on the bush walk."

I barely feel his good-bye kiss.

Don't Let Them See

Sandra Joy

One day at a time. That's what they all say. Just one day at a time.

The psychiatrist explained that the waves come in 20-minute cycles. So one day is a long time. In fact, that's 72 cycles to endure. Every. Single. Day. That's 72 opportunities to succeed or fail. That's 72 tests to pass. That's 72 times to doubt, question, and torture yourself. Another 72 times to hide it from the world.

Every day. Every single day. Will this ever end. Is this really worth it?

Yes!

Or so they say.

It's 6:53 and the kids will wake soon. Good mums are up before their kids, so it's time to get out of bed.

Ashleigh on the bus at 8:10.

Bella to playgroup at 8:20.

John to TAFE at 8:50.

Home by 9:20.

Then what?

Focus, woman, focus! I put one foot deliberately onto the floor. Today I will not drink. Today I will survive. They will not know how I really feel. And I will look normal.

Two feet on the floor. Shoulders back. Dressing gown on. You've got this.

Ashleigh is the first one awake. She meets me in the kitchen as I pour the water into my coffee.

"Hi darling." The words sound jittery, but I don't think she notices. Try again. "What's on today? Anything special?"

"Nah," she offers, "just another dumb test."

"Why..." I start to ask why she didn't tell me, but maybe she did. I can't appear to have forgotten yet another school event. "Why is it dumb?" Nice recovery woman!

After a while, Bella wanders into the kitchen and I let her wake up properly before seeking a hug. She is the least affectionate of the three, probably because touch is something she has had very little of. Life has many phases and the children are always the victims.

I have to wake John for TAFE. He chose to become a carpenter and I am so proud of him, but teenagers seem to need more sleep than any other age group. I sit gently on the edge of his bed and just look at his face. Oh, the hurt he has suffered. The pain he has felt.

I'm so sorry my darling. If I could take it all back, I would. You are so strong and so mature but for all the wrong reasons. I am so sorry. I wish I could go back to when it was just you and me. We were a great team. My best mate. John, I love you so much.

Part of me is tempted to let him sleep. To stay in his paradise free from reality, but I know he wants to go to TAFE. After all, his apprenticeship is his ticket to freedom. With that he has a title, a purpose, an income, a career. A reason to live. And a means of escape.

I yell at myself silently. It was not all my fault! Now shut up and put on a brave face. You've got this.

"Wakey wakey, rise and shine. Come on Johnno, it's getting up time." That's been his alarm since he was less than a year old.

When I return to the kitchen, with the promise that John will be there soon, Ashleigh is already making toast and has the cereal and milk on the table. I watch with sadness at the capability of one so young. This five-year-old is as familiar in the kitchen as I am, maybe more so — and not because I was such a great mum that I taught her. No, when you're hungry and your dad's nowhere around and your mother is drunk, you learn to fend for yourself.

She'll go far. She will succeed at anything she does. She is so capable. But I want her to have a childhood. I want her to play and laugh. But no, she's too busy being mum to her siblings. I'm grateful to her and angry at myself for this situation.

The tears well. I hate myself for causing my kids to grow up so fast. They're so young.

Stop it! Get a grip! It's 7:25 so you can collapse in two hours. Not now. Not in front of them. They don't need to pick you up again.

"Ashleigh, look at you darling. You are amazing! What can I do to help? Would you like me to get the plates? Butter the toast? Thank you so much for making breakfast." And I lean in to hug her.

"No, Mum. It's fine."

As I open the cupboard door to retrieve bowls and plates, my eyes are drawn to one item only. That glass. Everything else is opaque, but that one glass is crystal clear. The wave is back. That glass is the perfect size and shape for a double shot of bourbon, two ice cubes and just the right amount of coke. That glass has survived many a fun time. Others have broken but that one remains. My friend. Stop it. It's just a glass. In fact, if it's a problem, get rid of it. I can't throw it out now though, Ashleigh would see me do that and know I have a problem. I don't have a problem. I am sober. It's just a glass.

I steadily take four plates and bowls to the table. Then I turn back for the cutlery, but notice Ashleigh has them in one hand and the buttered toast in the other. Did I just lose time again or does she work really fast?

"Sorry, darling. I was going to do that for you."

"It's okay, Mum. Stop stressing."

That's my cue to shut up, so I smile on the outside and kick myself on the inside. I will not let her see the tears. I will not.

~

Even from the driveway, the house always seems the quietest when I arrive back after the morning school run. As I pause to look, the old rush of excitement returns – six hours until they're home. That's three hours to drink, two to sleep and sober up, one to shower and wake up before I go and get them. It's a routine I know well.

Not today. Not any more. I hope. That's the plan.

One day at a time.

Today is a new day. Today I have a new plan. One hour of cleaning, then one hour of reading. Lunch, phone my sister, then watch a DVD. Nothing major, nothing stressful. One day my life will be useful again, but for now I survive.

The next time I look at the clock, it tells me it's 11:15 – time for another coffee. While the water boils I review my morning achievements. Washing up done. Beds made. Towels folded and put away. That was a very productive morning. Well done me!

I sit down with my book and coffee and feel the wave again. The second mouthful tastes like bourbon mixed with diet Pepsi, yuk, and I know my taste buds are still out of whack.

When the phone rings I am surprised to see the caller is my niece, Karen.

"Hey Kaz, how are you?"

"I ... I ... Pete's ..."

I know the voice. I know the history. I don't need any more information.

"Where are you? I'm on my way!"

"Thank … you. Um … the Alby. Room 12."

"Don't move."

I leave my coffee and book where they are, grab my bag and head to the Albion Hotel to help my niece. At least that drunk hasn't put her in hospital again. I only hope I can convince her to leave him *this* time.

~

Like always, Kaz is restless as she slides through the phases of anger, hurt and guilt. I watch from my seat on the bed, assessing the limp, the welts and the bruises as each of her movements reveals another place his fist connected. Our words are the same as so many times before, but I hear myself being more forceful now. Not because the assault was any worse, not because I thought there was more chance of her staying away. No, this time, for the first time, I am seeing the situation through sober eyes and I *know,* I now *believe,* that there is life without alcohol.

Just then, the motherly instinct kicks in, and I check my watch for the first time since we started talking. It's 2:20 and there is no way I can get to the school in time, and no way I want to leave

Karen without her promising to leave Pete for real.

I call my neighbour and ask her to pick up the kids. She knows Karen, so I don't have to say too much before she understands why. "Oh, and my phone's dying, so if you need me we are at the Alby, Room 12."

Kids safe, I can focus on Karen again.

"I'm starving, can we go get some lunch?"

"Sure," I reply, "my shout. Where do you wanna go?"

"Downstairs? Toby still makes great burgers."

Downstairs. In the restaurant. Attached to the bar.

No problem, I can do this. This is about Karen, not me. I'm sober. I'm fine. I had been so focused on her that I actually forgot I was in a pub.

Like clockwork, the temptation flows every 20 minutes. The iced glasses, the bourbons disguised with coke; wines and beers. NO!

I don't know this cashier, but I order two burgers and add a plate of chips to share. While my back is turned, Karen wanders over to the bar and returns with two drinks — a beer for her and a bourbon and coke for me.

I cannot count the messages flying through my head right now. You can't offend her. Just say no. This is about her. You've got this. One won't matter. Oh, I can almost taste the sweetness, the heat…

"Thanks Kaz, but I'm not drinking any more. I'll just have water."

I did it. I actually said no to a drink! So proud!

To my surprise, Karen doesn't make a big deal out of it. Maybe under different circumstances she would have, but today she is too upset and distracted to really notice. She takes it back to the bar – I'm not sure what they'll do with it, I've never *returned* a drink before.

~

As we finish our lunch, the waiter comes and clears out plates.

"Hi Kay, you had a phone call."

I start to stand, quickly assuming it is my neighbour, and something is wrong with the kids.

His hand goes out to stop me. "No, it's ok, he hung up."

My puzzled frown invites more information.

"Your son, John, rang and asked if you were here. I started to say, 'yeah hang on mate, I'll get her.' But he hung up."

My mouth drops to my heart. My heart drops to my stomach.

I'm at a pub and the kids know. No matter what they're told, they will assume I'm drinking.

I *have* to get home.

They *have* to see that I didn't drink.

"Karen, I am really sorry, but I have to go."

That too, was easier than I expected.

"Can I come with you?"

"Of course! But we have to go *now*. Are you getting your stuff or coming back later?"

We race up to room 12, but time seems to be in slow motion as we throw her few belongings into her overnight bag.

I am desperate to see my kids. For them to see me. Sober.

~

Checking out takes forever. Driving takes forever. Reaching my kids takes forever.

When I open that front door and see the three of them huddled on the lounge, John reading to his younger sisters, my heart stops. They all look up, not with excitement, but with the familiar terror — expecting me to stagger in drunk. But this time I'm sober.

John is the first to meet my eyes and his head does a double take as he realises that I'm not drunk.

Tears fall as I watch him slowly remove his arms from Ashleigh and Bella's shoulders and say, "Mummy's home."

He walks cautiously toward me without taking his eyes from mine. The smile on both our faces grow as he approaches.

"Thank you, mum. You've got this. I love you so much."

———

The Farewell

George Graves

She froze. Hand near her face. No movement. In the middle of the wave, her arm stopped moving and just stayed there, fixed. The moment when she smiled, just a quick short smile, had passed. The warmth of her expression was replaced by something blank; something devoid of feeling. Numb. Or was it a touch of sadness? He could not tell from this far away. Perhaps what he saw was only a reflection of his own feelings.

As he had climbed the stairs to board the plane, he had stopped at the top and, before entering, had turned around. She was standing beside her mother, not very far away from the plane, to one side of the small cream-coloured concrete hut that formed the terminal at that little airport. When he had waved, she had taken one step forward, it seemed almost involuntarily, and had waved back. And then she stopped.

Looking out the window, he could see her, standing, still, no movement, her arms beside her now, her head slightly downcast. The plane's engines began to warm up and as it began to move, she turned and walked away.

The plane was climbing now. He was surprised he could make out the house where he had stayed, together with the small lake behind it. The plane turned and headed over the lagoon where he had seen the coral and so many fish, and then the harbour. The lush tropical green of the Papua New Guinean town was suddenly replaced by the turquoise of the ocean. The town was gone.

~

A full year had passed. He had moved into a flat in a small country town in northwestern New South Wales, where he worked in a bank. Life went back to 'normal', whatever that was. No one, not a soul, had asked him about what had happened and he didn't bring it up with his friends. To them, it simply seemed that he had forgotten her.

He enjoyed living and working in the town, even if the customers' comments were a bit predictable. Yes, *it certainly is a beautiful day*. No, *it doesn't look like rain*. Yes, *it was unusual the way the roly-poly blew down the main street. Some of those tumbleweeds must have been three feet wide.*

He played squash and swam in the pool. Swimming in the river that bisected the town was not an option as it was usually only a flat expanse of sand, except when it flooded. Then nobody went near the raging torrent.

The balls were fun. Once, some pipers came from a nearby town. Before entering the hall for the beginning of the ball, they marched down the main street, their kilts swinging to the rhythm of the music, the sound of the bagpipes drowning out the feeble efforts of the dogs and cars. The laddies, dressed in their penguin outfits, the lassies in their finest dresses, danced, ate dinner, flirted, and danced some more until the early hours of the morning.

He thought of her now and then. Well, truthfully, a bit more than that. Once he met her unexpectedly at a friend's place down in the city. She happened to be there with a male friend of hers. He felt awkward, did not say much, wished her all the best, and left.

Sitting in a quiet park a few miles from town, beside the non-existent stream, he drifted off into a daydream, thinking about his time on the island. He noticed he was doing this more often as her birthday approached.

Sometimes he thought of the time when he had been living on the island for more than a year, when his term of employment had come to a close. It was then he had time to explore, to walk along beaches, visit the mountains again and snorkel in the crystal-clear waters of the lagoon where the coral grew in abundance and the fish of so many different colours swam in never-ending schools.

Now, he was thinking about her and, in particular, the first time he had seen her. While the sun, high overhead, scorched the park and the farms, the scene drifted into his mind.

He remembered how it happened. No longer was he in the small country town, he was there again. On the island ...

He was tired. The heat and humidity only confirmed what he already knew; he was out of condition. While leaning against the rough bark of a tree, he decided it was time to rest awhile.

When he sat down, the long grass seemed almost cool to his touch. Where the sun blazed down, the grass was a vivid green. But here, under the tree, most of the harshness of the sunlight was subdued by the overhanging branches.

It was then he noticed how beautiful the scene was in front of him. A low branch hid some of the sky and framed the view, almost as artists often paint a limb across a portion of the top of a painting.

To the left palm trees reached up to the sky, some at rather odd angles, all with the same greyish brown trunks, the sedate green foliage on top and a few brown coconuts.

Ahead, past the tufts of grass that clung to the soil before it fell away to the sand, the beach flowed down to the water's edge. Here, the unbroken line of a wave moved slowly to the shore, to flop down on the sand. In a while, the ocean, seeming to be almost overcome with the heat also, gathered up enough energy to form another little wave which slowly moved to the shore, to flop down as before. The water, crystal clear, changed from mid-blue in the bay to a paler hue near the horizon.

He was struck by how quiet the place was — no bird calls, no voices, just the subdued splash of waves now and then. Obviously two people had recently walked past where he was sitting, down to the beach, their footprints disappearing to the left. The rest of the sand was smooth.

Far to the right, the beach faded out to a headland. Back from the beach were the usual palms, but also more shrubs and other trees. Hidden almost from view was one of the typical huts of the area — rectangular, the sides made from woven bamboo, with a thatched roof. In front, just visible, was a hollow log, a slit running lengthways along the top. It was a drum beaten by the locals for calling other villagers, for ceremonies or just when they had a fun time together.

He felt tranquil and relaxed and, with the heat — his mind drifted away.

Startled. In front of him, halfway to the water's edge, was a woman. He must have been day-dreaming and so had not seen her before.

He didn't recognise her. She was new to the town. Don't get many tourists wandering about by themselves so she was probably a friend of one of the expats.

From the shade, he could watch her without her noticing him. She was facing a little away, walking along slowly, looking at the sand. He guessed she may have been in her early or mid-twenties (who is game to be certain about a woman's age nowadays), a little below average height and quite pretty. Under a light blue translucent sun-frock, she wore a red bikini. Not a brash 'notice-I-am-here' colour but a subdued red, almost maroon. What struck him most was her hair: almost straight, it hung halfway down her back, a light brown colour, golden where the sun shone directly on it.

She stopped and stooped to pick up a seashell, and her hair fell past her face. With a brush of her left hand and a small flick of her head, it was back in place, sitting on her shoulders and lying on her back.

She turned a little towards where he was sitting and he froze. For some reason he felt guilty about watching her, almost like a voyeur. Should he stand and announce himself? He could now see the small smile on her face and noticed how beautiful she was. Her expression was one of thoughtfulness but, at the same time, contentedness.

Suddenly there was 'crack' behind him. Surprised by the noise, he quickly turned around and looked for anything that could have caused it but could find nothing unusual. It was probably just a falling coconut. All was quiet again, and as far as he could tell, they were the only two people anywhere near the beach.

He turned back to find the beach empty. Was it a dream – had he imagined her? Where was she? Then he noticed the footprints leading off to the right along the beach and up into the palms.

He looked back to where she had stopped and then he saw, lying on the sand, glistening white in the harsh sunshine, the seashell.

~

The town was only small and so it was fairly easy to find her, 'accidentally' meeting her in the one and only cafe. She smiled when he told her of his voyeurism, waiting for days for a gorgeous young woman to walk along the beach. Then he told her the truth; he was a bit absent-minded and day-dreamy and he had been there, for the first time, for perhaps half an hour when she walked past.

They began to go places together, enjoying each other's company. He had never met someone so warm and friendly. Before leaving the island, each gave the other their address and phone number so they could continue to see each other back home. He smiled when he noticed they lived only a few suburbs apart in the same city.

~

Oh! I so loved the time I was with you, for the year, back in Australia. It was so much fun. We enjoyed being together, watching movies, listening to orchestras, going for walks and having dinners together. Remember the movie we saw the first time we went to the drive-in? Wasn't it marvellous? Perhaps the company had made it such a wonderful night. We visited friends and went to church together. It felt so good to be close to you. One time we lay on a rug in a park by a creek and watched the clouds float by, the sun streaming between the trees, forming soft shadows on the grass. I was so relaxed; probably the most relaxed I have ever been in my life.

Do you remember the time we went fishing? That did not turn out so well, did it? Tangled lines, a shower of rain, damp, and not a fish between the two of us. At least the fish had a great day. They should have been much fatter from the number of prawns we fed them! We did get one critter though. A crab. It ran, scurried, or whatever crabs do, around the bottom of the boat, with you squealing when it approached your bare toes, until I scooped it out of the boat with the blade of an oar. Then the motor broke down and I had to row back to the hire place. Initially we both tried to row, you on one oar, me on the other, but we could not get it right. Each of us was trying to row as quickly as we could and we kept going in circles. We both laughed as we went around again and again. We then decided that perhaps only one of us should row. I drew the short straw. We certainly had something to tell our friends, didn't we?

What was the most enjoyable? Getting to know you and being trusted by you? Listening to the music of your voice and being entranced by your enthusiasm for life? Sitting on the lounge next to you, listening to music? All the trivia of the world faded away as we cuddled each other, the sounds of the orchestra from the home-made record player drifting over us. Brahms and Beethoven, Schubert and Mozart. Concertos and symphonies. Oh, I miss that.

We had something to celebrate, didn't we, and you wanted to show your mum and dad something special. So, we decided to have a holiday back on the island where we met, where I had my first glimpse of you on the beach. Is it only a month ago we organised to come here? It seems a lifetime has passed. How I would like to undo the last couple of weeks, to have that time again, to change what happened. And here I am now, on a plane by myself, going home.

~

I'm beginning to get old, he thought as he peered at his face in the mirror. All the hair is white now and the ginger beard is mottled grey. Oh well, I suppose it had to happen. I don't remember getting old. It kind of crept up on me. I can still get around better than most of the old codgers here. I only need my walking stick; not like some of them with their Zither, or Zimmer, or whatever, frames. Oh, I'm bored witless here. Have I had breakfast? I don't know. I suppose so. What will I do? Go and sit with the rest of them and watch some mind-numbing thing on TV? I wonder what day it is. Yes, I know, I'll look at my watch — it has the day on it. Why did I think of her again? My glasses — yes, there they are, beside the bed. Now, I see, it's Saturday. Oh good. My daughter or son may come today. But did they come last week? I don't know. If they did, they won't come today. But I would so love to see each of them, and my daughter brings me such interesting things to read.

Funny that I thought of her again. It seems to have been a while now. I wonder if she ever thinks of me. Probably not. Probably hasn't for sixty years. Why would she? Didn't think of her for years and years at one stage. The memories seem so mixed up now. They run into each other and some do not even seem to belong to me. It is as though they are someone else's.

Dreamt of her last night. So strange. A dream of when I was young and she was young too. We were messing about in a boat. I'm older than her. Seven days, I think. Yes, seven days older.

I suppose I had better go out and be with the others. Nurse has been telling me to get out of my room more. Watch TV with the others, she said. And while staring at the screen, all the thoughts keep running around in my head. I wonder if she still loves music?

Do I have time before I go? Yes, just for a moment. Where is it? Yes, found it, beside the seashell, at the back of my socks. Oh, so beautiful still. The emerald shining so brightly between the cluster of six diamonds. It never would have worked out, would it, I murmur softly to myself. Her mother said it was just infatuation, that's all. I hope her life has been wonderful. Oh. A tear. So silly after so long. Mustn't let nurse see me like this. Put it away now. Where's my stick? There, by the door. Better go out and be with the rest of them. Best if others don't know what I'm thinking about. Mustn't let nurse know. Probably thinks I am crazy. Perhaps I am. Oh well, off to the TV. Wonder what's on. Oh, it's tennis — that's not too bad.

Broken Chords

Rina Robinson

The Dancer

She leaves her chair
And moves to the centre of the room.
She takes a step.
Then another: then totters some more.
It is not pretty.
But in her mind
The music swells and she soars
Graceful, beautiful,
A ballerina again.

The Singer

He tries to rise
From the wheelchair's irreverent
    constraint,
A patchwork of harmony
At last, before the swan song.
His crestfallen aspect
Is reversed for a moment.
The baritone voice surprises,
Rich, powerful,
The song he remembers.

The Judge

He raises his arm,
A tangled salute to the day.
A haunted Solomon,
Yesterday's arbiter of power.
Yet bedevilled brains
Overtake the apathy
And face the jury.
Harmonious verdict,
His future epitaph.

---

* This poem was awarded a Commendation Prize in the Roland Robinson Literary Award for 1996 and appeared in the anthology, *Lines from a Lakeside City* the same year. It was reprinted in *HPA Magazine*, issue 4 2019.

The Fishing Trip

Tony Lang

William Billings, known around Wangi town as Billy, stood at the kitchen door and surveyed his family — his wife Irene and their three hungry teenagers. The boys had their cutlery in the 'ready' position.

"Good evening, wifey dear. Good evening, handsome sons!" he called. Irene returned the welcoming smile. The boys replied with a series of unintelligible grunts.

Billy settled his ample bulk on his chair at the kitchen table and picked up his cutlery. As soon as he and Irene commenced, so did their sons, with the frenzied alacrity of the starving.

Billy indicated the boys with his fork. "Just look at them, Irene — finest kids you'll ever see, and all as healthy as young colts."

Billy's prominent jowls quivered with pride.

Irene smiled as she watched them. Terry — Sparky to his brothers — the eldest, soon to finish his electrician's apprenticeship. She looked over to Peter, or Stumpy as his brothers called him because of his stocky build. Smart boy and apprenticed to a carpenter. She glanced over at Ian — or Prof to his siblings — first year uni, studying law and loving it. Irene smiled to herself, recalling it was she who arranged their apprenticeships and Ian's university career. Billy's a good husband and father, she thought, and Lake Macquarie Council pays its outside staff well. But his thoughts were only for the present moment.

Billy waited until the initial feeding frenzy had subsided, then banged his spoon on the table. The boys stopped eating and looked up.

"Good news, boys — I've managed to get us another boat. Not like the last one. This one's a real beauty! Isn't that great news?"

The great news was greeted with silence.

Terry said, "Dad — all your beaut boat buys have been anything but great news. On that last fishing trip we had to swim for it. Luckily the Swansea rescue crew saw us!"

Their father was nodding. "True, true. It was unfortunate that the planks opened up in that old wooden boat. But you gotta look on the bright side, boy. I mean, we got our names in the *Newcastle Herald*!"

"And what about the boat before that?" Ian broke in. "That night-fishing trip ... part of the stern broke off and took the outboard with it — we had to row for miles in the dark. We nearly got run down by the *Wangi Queen*!"

Again Billy nodded. "True — but what a great piece of navigation we did in the dark! I think we all learned a lot that night. You gotta look for all the positives in life, Ian. Anyway, I didn't bring youse boys up to be pessimists! You gotta look on the bright side because all these situations teach us something. Now, because those other boats were bits of lemons — "

"You got squeezed good and proper each time," Ian whispered.

Billy ignored the comment and sniggers. "I have now managed to get a fantastic buy off a friend of a friend, who's given a water-tight promise that this boat is immaculate. He got it at a clearance sale. It's a tinny, fourteen feet long, new paint job inside and out, with a twenty-horsepower donk on the back, and it's on a trailer. The only thing is, the outboard is an oldie but it's a goodie. It's been thoroughly overhauled. Great price too." He tapped the side of his nose. "Mate's rates. It's not what you know but who you know."

Terry rolled his eyes. "Where've I heard those words before?" he muttered.

"Anyway, I pick it up on Saturday," Billy added. "I've got bait ordered. We've got our rods. Let's give those fish a nudge on Saturday afternoon! Irene, make sure the pan is hot for when we get home. Fish for tea!"

The boys looked at each other. Peter was about to speak but his mother beat him to it.

"I'd like you boys to go with your father. You can keep an eye on one another, and you never know, you might even land a fish or two." She was thankful the boys were now old enough to watch out for their father.

The boys nodded. Dad on his own could end up a problem.

Saturday morning dawned bright and clear and the weatherman cheerfully forecast a mild, sunny day. The boys were disappointed. They'd been hoping for wind and rain and even cyclonic conditions — anything to put the kybosh on their father's enthusiastic fishing plans.

They were at the Wangi boat ramp when Billy arrived with the boat. The boys looked at it with interest. It looked every bit as good as their father had promised.

"Maybe the old man managed to pull it off this time," Ian murmured to the others.

Billy swung the vehicle around and backed the trailer into the water.

"Right, let's get the boat in," he called. "I can almost hear those big bream sizzling in the pan!"

Their father's never-ending enthusiasm was infectious. They set to with a will.

The motor burst into life at the first turn of the key. Soon they were creaming across the lake towards the haunt of big fish: the 'drop-off' near Swansea channel, where the shallow sandy bottom suddenly drops off into deeper water.

Terry was up near the bow, in the wind and sun and salt spray.

"This is great dad!" he called. "Looks like you got it right at las..."

The outboard suddenly coughed and spluttered, then stopped. Deprived of its forward thrust, the boat began to wallow in the slight chop.

"Don't worry boys!" Billy called. "The bloke I bought it off told me it does that sometimes. All I have to do is give it a bit of extra choke."

He fiddled briefly and hit the starter. There was a reluctant whirring, then silence. Billy tried it again. And again – silence.

Billy glared at the engine in disgust. He picked up his rod, baited the line, made a cast and leaned the rod against the side of the boat.

"Oh well, I might as well see if I can catch something on the drift. Hey – we're drifting the wrong way. Better chuck out the anchor, Ian."

Ian picked up the anchor and heaved it over the side. The rope and chain streaked out. Billy watched it.

"Hey, Ian," he called anxiously, "check to make sure the chain at this end is fastened to the boat – oh, hell!" Horrified, they all watched as anchor, line and chain disappeared into the depths below.

"Why didn't you make sure the anchor chain was fastened to the cleat, Prof?" Terry yelled. "Now we don't have an anchor!"

"Now, now boys," Billy placated, "cut it out – no need to do the block over a simple accident. It could have happened to any of us. Let's use it as another lesson in seamanship: always make sure the anchor is attached to the boat! I think I saw some oars. We can row back, no worries!"

Terry found the oars down each side of the boat.

"Gee, dad, these oars don't look very strong — they're made of plastic! They look like they belong to a canoe, or a small dinghy."

Billy ran an eye over them. "Yep, son — I'd say you're right. They certainly didn't come with the original gear. Still, they're all we've got, so we'll have to make do. Right, boys — we'll take turns to row us back to Wangi Point. At least we've got the rowlocks to put 'em in. Terry and Peter — you're first on the oars. One each side. Off you go!"

The boys settled themselves on each side of the boat and started rowing. Slowly the boat came about and started towards Wangi Point.

Two minutes later there was a yell. Terry was on his back in the bottom of the boat.

"Dad!" he yelled, "the blade of the oar snapped off!"

A few seconds later there was another yell — this time from Peter:

"Dad! This oar's done the same — we're oar-less!"

They watched helplessly as the boat recommenced its inevitable drift towards Swansea channel.

Billy scratched his head. "What are we gunna do now?" He sat on one of the seats and pondered the situation for a couple of minutes.

Suddenly he sat up. "Got it! Are all youse boys wearing your thongs?"

They looked at him. "Yeah," said Peter. "Why?"

Their father pointed to his feet. "So am I. Each of you take one off and slip it onto your hand."

They stared at him. "What?"

"Just do it. Peter and Terry, put your thong on your right hand. Ian, put yours on your left hand. I will too. Now listen, boys — you've seen those Maori canoes where the Maori crews have those short paddles that they dig into the water. Now you can pretend to be Maori paddlers, but your thongs are the paddles. Get to it!"

They paddled strenuously for ten minutes. "Gosh, dad — this is hard work!" Ian called, panting. "Can't we stop for a bit?"

"Of course we can't! We'll lose all the ground we've made up if we stop — hullo — that line I cast out ... the rod's bobbing about! I think I've caught a fish."

Billy turned and reeled in the line.

"Got one ... Ah — too bad — too small. I'll have to toss him back — oops — I dropped him, getting him off the hook. He's in the boat somewhere. Can't stop — we gotta keep going!"

Slowly Wangi Point shore grew closer.

Billy was sweating with exertion. "When we get back, a couple of youse boys take the outboard off the back. I'm gunna get it properly serviced."

With sighs of relief the paddlers heard the keel slide onto sand. Soon the boat was at the ramp. Terry and Peter took the motor off and leaned it on the fish-cleaning bench, ready to put in the ute.

They'd just put the boat on the trailer when a man approached.

"G'day, boys. Been having some fun on the water?"

"Had a bit of trouble with the motor," Billy told him. "We had to paddle back."

"Catch any fish?"

"Nah, mate — nuthin."

"I'm from NSW Fisheries and Wildlife." He flashed a badge. "Mind if I have a look?"

He jumped up onto the trailer and into the boat. In a moment he found the undersize bream.

"This yours?"

There was a guilty silence.

The man's expression hardened. "You realise it's an offence to take undersize fish?"

"Yeah, but — "

"I'll need your names, addresses and fishing licences. There may be a fine, and I'll be confiscating your fishing gear."

"What?" Billy roared, "you can't do that!"

"'fraid I can, mate. It's the law."

Just then Terry came running up. "Dad — the motor's gone! Some mongrel's walked off with the outboard!"

The boys had never seen their father so angry. Profanities rent the air as he brought down numerous curses on the head of the outboard motor thief.

On the way home, Billy returned the boat, wanting his money back but the yard was empty.

"It wasn't a clearance sale — it was a 'get the money-and clear-out-sale!'" he declared.

Back home, Irene greeted her family as they trudged into the house. She noted their doleful expressions. It was the usual story, she thought, when all her boys went fishing.

"The pan's on, boys, and the fat's sizzling! Where are the fish?"

The glum silence told her she was right.

"I thought that might happen, so I bought some fresh flathead fillets." She went off to the kitchen, chortling.

As they ate, Billy said, "I think we might give away the fishing for a while, boys. Now I've been talking to a bloke who knows a bloke in Wallsend who wants to sell his nice little campervan. He says it's in top nick ..."

He would have said more, but the yells drowned him out.

Magic of a River

Anita Richardson

Rivers have always held a fascination for me and a river trip in the wilds of Borneo appealed to my sense of adventure. My friend Max, however, would have preferred to stay at a luxury beachfront resort in Bali. After some lively discussion and necessary medical precautions, we took off by plane, for Balikpapan in Southern Borneo. Our hotel was like a cardboard stage prop. Outside it looked fabulous. Flowing, floodlit fountains and tropical greenery. Inside nothing worked.

"These lights don't work and there's no water in the taps," Max complained.

However, breakfast was delicious and we enjoyed omelettes cooked to our taste right in front of us.

We set off by four-wheel drive to a spot on the Mahakam River where we were to embark on a journey upstream into the interior of Borneo. The advertisement for the trip had mentioned a luxury river cruise. On the wharf two giant, painted wooden serpents gazed out over the wide river. A sparkling white cabin cruiser was tied up alongside so I made towards it, anticipating air conditioning, luxury and a welcome glass of anything!

"No, no, that's not ours," stated the guide, who then steered us towards a smaller, somewhat odd vessel, which actually sat below the level of the wharf.

"Surely this isn't the craft we are going on?" I questioned, as I stood, a bewildered tourist in my beaded sunhat, floral skirt and sunnies.

Our guide advised that the other passengers had cancelled. He had been forced to change to a smaller boat. Max was horrified. He wanted to catch the next plane home.

If the adventure was to proceed, there was no option other than to abandon the prospect of luxurious comfort aboard the cruiser. I threw caution to the wind and without even a backward glance at the other launch, jumped aboard the little river boat. Miserable Max clambered aboard too.

The little craft proved sturdy. Her crew of five were fun to be with, proud of the river and their boat. The Chinese chef turned out to be excellent.

There was one cabin up top with an extended viewing deck and two folding chairs. We slept in the cabin on a mattress, cocooned inside mosquito nets into which we crawled, smothered in repellent. The crew slept on the lower deck as did any number of their relatives, who seemed to appear each night for a lift upriver.

It was stiflingly hot and humid, however the breeze coming off the river was refreshing.

In order to use the bathroom during the night we had to use a ladder to the lower level. You needed to step down through the air across the missing last six rungs to land precariously amongst whoever might be asleep at the bottom. It was a case of look before you leap! Max did not take kindly to this little exercise.

The shower was enthralling! There must have been a suction hose down to the bottom of the river to bring the water on board. I couldn't tell if I was any cleaner for showering or not, such was the colour of the water.

The Chinese chef was a treasure, cooking up a variety of meals and every day a batch of deep-fried banana fritters for an afternoon snack – simply scrumptious. Max scored a beer every time a meal was served but I only managed to get coffee. He smiled each time he sipped his beer.

We sat in the rickety chairs each morning watching the constant traffic on the river. The boats were built entirely by hand and some were really long. People crowded on board, along with drums of petrol, timber, livestock, fighting cocks in cages, chickens and pigs.

The river was starting to weave its spell on Max, who became a little happier as each day passed. At intervals along the river we came across triangular shaped fishing nets of turquoise green suspended from bamboo poles. Perched atop the poles were beautiful little kingfishers waiting patiently for their next meal.

Other nets were hand cast by men standing upright in their canoes. As they moved in a rhythmic pattern, they seemed to be at one with nature and a sense of timelessness prevailed.

At night we sat on the little deck sipping wine and watched the prawning boats work the river. Twinkling lights ashore enhanced the scene, the sky simply wondrous, stars shimmering like diamonds and the river luminous.

The scenery constantly changed. Some houses were built high on poles on the banks of the river. Others floated on wooden pontoons of logs lashed together. During monsoon season the Mahakam could be treacherous sweeping many homes away. The people simply rebuilt.

Wooden jetties extended out into the river with a sort of shower facility at the end. Families lined up next to each other carrying towels on their shoulders enjoying a communal, chatty time. Naked children flipped themselves into the river.

Some women carried baskets of washing on their heads. I couldn't picture myself throwing our weekly wash onto my shoulders and strolling down to our local creek. Other women stood waist high in the water gathering mussels which they placed in floating wicker buckets.

We left the boat to explore a floating village. The entire village was built on floating logs but it was quite strong in construction and firm underfoot. There were no clotheslines for washing so clothing was spread out on low hedges which surrounded each dwelling.

Raised high off the ground, fish dried in the sun on bamboo slats. A scraggy cat looked longingly upwards, the bamboo supports too smooth for him to climb.

Another time we visited a shore village. Cute little monkeys were kept as pets but, because they could be aggressive, they needed to be chained. The chains were long enough so the monkeys could run around. That evening we saw a monkey who had escaped his chain and was leaping about in the overhead wiring. I felt frightened for him. The whole village was out trying to cajole him down with long poles and calling out to him. Electricity is only switched on in the evenings for short periods. It was due to come on at six o'clock. As it was close to six we turned the nearest corner and did not look back. We would not take the chance of seeing the little creature fried alive!

As the river narrowed, it became evident that soon there would not be enough flow of water for us to proceed. However, there was no need for concern as the skipper had prepared for this. From out of thin air three canoes appeared. Each canoe had a canopy overhead and a motor driven propeller at the rear.

The locals call the canoes *mudskippers* and that's exactly what they did for the next part of the journey, mud flying in all directions! Every now and then even the mud ran out and we tramped on foot with the men shouldering the canoes. Max looked kind of pitiful in his safari suit covered in mud, but he soldiered on. Eventually we got to a good stretch of water which took us to a jetty. A scramble through more mud to reach the jetty and a short trek through the jungle to our first longhouse and, after all that, we were looking forward to a decent shower and a comfortable bed.

The longhouse looked aged and in front of the building stood a row of carved totems. We were asked to remove our shoes out of respect for the gods but, once inside, we discovered that we were walking on a dirt floor, so the removal of footwear didn't really make a great deal of difference.

Our room sported a four-poster bed under a velvet canopy. A cubicle seemed to be a shower of sorts but it turned out to contain only a bucket of river water with a ladle. There was a gap between the wall and the roof, so out came the repellent again. We cleaned our teeth with whisky which Max conjured up from some hidden place.

We woke to a rooster which crowed so loud as to deafen us. He was perched on a wall just outside. He almost crowed for the last time that morning!

After that wonderful night's sojourn, we went inland travelling by separate four-wheel drives. Max went with one driver, and I went with another. After a while I looked behind, and there was no sign of the second vehicle. My driver spoke no English so I couldn't get him to turn off his blaring radio. My nerves were getting edgy. Passing through grasses head high beside the vehicles and with no really visible track in sight, I kept thinking, *thank goodness there are no lions in Borneo.* And then I remembered the tigers!

At last we arrived at the Dayak village set in cleared jungle and sporting an even taller longhouse. The Dayaks greeted us warmly, painted our faces and arms with yellow ochre. They danced a graceful ceremonial dance in a circle. Max and I danced with them. They have made their home in the jungle away from civilisation and hunted with blowpipes using poison-tipped darts. Max had a go at a blowpipe, much to his delight.

The Dayaks were small in stature but very fit. The men wore necklaces and armbands made of tiger teeth. They looked splendid in ceremonial dress which was woven from grasses dyed with tints from seeds. Max had sweets for the children and he was almost knocked over in the rush. As we left, they placed necklaces of seed beads around our necks and wished us a safe trip home.

The visit to the Dayaks was the high point of the journey. It was a glimpse of a people existing in an isolated area. There was no sign of television or books, but the fact that we were there meant they were trying to connect with the outside world.

For our return trip, it was back to the river. There were a few more excursions in the canoes up little side streams. We went early in the morning when mists were thick and saw tracks in the mud of what looked like crocodiles. I felt a bit too close to nature then.

Sometimes it is interesting to take a less beaten track. This trip upriver was nothing like we had imagined. We'd been close to tropical rainforest every day, seeing people living simple but happy lives, while facing great adversity at times. I couldn't visualise the river swollen and angry but the people of Borneo live with that and the struggle is ongoing.

Max and I came to the conclusion that there probably never was a larger cruiser with extra passengers but it really didn't matter because we had actually enjoyed a memorable trip on a fascinating waterway. Our memories now hold the magic of a river.

Deep Water

Pam Garfoot

"Three schooners of draught, please mate."

Greg's head goes down immediately as he lines up the glasses. He starts pulling the beers and doesn't look up. No eye contact, no small talk. Greg is used to seeing lots of t-shirts and hi-vis shirts. And worse, many big bellies. But anything from the neck down is fine by him. It's amazing he didn't get the sack after his first fortnight here. He's not good at chatting to the customers, but despite his failings he *is* pretty good at getting things done quickly.

On outings with his mates on a night off, deep conversation is not one of his priorities either. Talk revolves around the results of the latest footy round, what's going wrong with Tom's boat or Jason's ute, and whether Hungry Jacks or Maccas does a better burger. As far as Greg is concerned, shallow is good. He's a natural.

Beers poured, Greg works his way through a few more orders. Two white wines and a cider. Some light beers. A lemon-lime-and-bitters, a Coopers ale. Lots of bellies and a really skinny guy reeking of stale cigarette smoke.

Two of the guys in hi-vis share a joke when turning from the bar.

"The lights are on, but nobody's home," he hears one of them murmur, and they snigger. He lets it wash over him.

There's a momentary lull and he allows himself a brief glance across the bar towards the lounge bar and the bistro. It's a busy night with most tables and stools occupied. He sees a woman outlined against the eerie glow of the big screen on the far wall of the lounge bar. There's something he recognises in the familiar tilt of her head and the slightly upturned nose. With a lurch in his gut he realises it's Astrid. She's sitting amongst a small group of drinkers and turns to face her friends so that he can see only the gentle curve of her cheek in a three-quarter view. He feels sick inside and turns his attention back to his post.

A few anxious drinkers have begun to cluster at the bar. Greg fumbles pouring a couple of schooners and takes a minute, his back to the counter, to steady his shaking hands. From his left, he hears the snap of some clicking fingers and a terse, "Hey mate, down this end!"

He turns to cast a quick look down the far end of the bar. It's one of those city-types wearing a slim-cut shirt with a blue and white floral pattern. This guy has *actually* clicked his fingers. *Wanker.*

He decides to serve the two or three customers who have gathered in front of him before he moves down the end to serve the guy in the floral shirt. He's careful not to look up.

"Two margaritas, thanks," comes the order.

Margaritas. Double wanker.

He needs to ask one of the other barmen where the margarita glasses are, and while he's busy setting up the salt-rimmed edges for the cocktails – it takes a while – his mind moves to Astrid. How long has it been since she broke it off? Six months? Seven? Not that it was ever really *on*, but he liked to think they might be going somewhere. Not so Astrid, it seemed.

"Look Greg," she'd said in the pizzeria, the bench table a no-man's land between them and her pizza almost untouched. "I do like you ... but

I would need to like you a whole lot more if we were to keep seeing each other. I just can't seem to connect with you."

Greg had looked down at the train wreck of his meatlovers pizza and given a slight nod of his head. She was right. They weren't connecting. Did he really know how to?

"It's hard to get close, Greg, to someone who never reveals himself."

There might have been some pleading in her voice, a sort of unspoken invitation. He couldn't tell. And he couldn't meet her eyes. His lip quivered the tiniest bit, but Astrid didn't see — she was already turning to leave.

So it was over, after little more than a month. Greg wonders, now, if she ever even thinks of him.

Margarita guy pays for his cocktails and carries them confidently away towards the other room. Greg takes a break from the bar to clear some glasses even though it isn't supposed to be his job. The girls from the bistro are supposed to clear when they get the chance.

He moves towards the lounge bar, stacking up glasses over his shoulder, and steals a few glances in Astrid's direction. The crowd in there is growing. The steady hum of chatter and laughter comes from the lounge bar. A hens night is gathering momentum and they're blocking his line of sight. Yet he can sense her in the throng.

Then he catches sight of margarita guy working his way through the noisy women, holding the cocktail glasses aloft with a disdainful arrogance. He's heading in Astrid's direction.

Greg feels bile rise in his throat as he watches margarita guy push his way through to Astrid and extend one of the cocktails to her waiting hand. She smiles at him, and he leans in close to say something above the din of the raucous women off to his side. She laughs up at him.

A small crowd is gathering at the bar and making impatient comments to each other. Greg doesn't turn to them. He watches Astrid, though she seems not to have noticed him. He sets the glasses down at an empty table and pushes his way through the throng towards her.

A white-hot glow swells within him. As he draws near there is finally a small flicker of recognition from Astrid.

"My god. Greg." Her voice is small and uncertain. She looks across at her companion, then back at Greg.

Greg moves forward. Then, instead of approaching Astrid, he walks up to margarita guy. He says nothing but his body speaks for him. His right arm flexes with anger. It rises suddenly and he whacks margarita guy in his smarmy face.

Flesh-and-blood on flesh-and-blood.

The sickening sound reverberates through the swirling crowd. There are cries from the hens women. There's a sudden panicky retreat as they shrink back. Astrid's face is white over margarita guy's prone body.

Greg gasps and pants, but still he does not speak. He feels the firm grasp of hands on his shoulders. Voices threaten. Someone is crying. A siren begins to wail in the distance.

Another voice speaks but it must be inside Greg's head. *Shit, why did you explode like that*? *What have you done*? And Greg begins to think — he actually knows — it would have been a whole lot better if he'd let his feelings rise to the surface a long time ago.

Beneath the Gossip

James Horn

In early December 1926, reporters converged at the usually quiet Rickmansworth Station to descend upon my cousin Nancy Neele's family home, *Rheola*. It was almost impossible to shake them off. They had discovered that Nancy had been having an affair with the handsome and dashing WW1 Royal Flying Corps Officer, Colonel Archie Christie. He was still married to the extraordinarily popular murder mystery writer, Agatha Christie. And, Agatha was missing in very intriguing circumstances.

Cousin Nancy, born in 1899, was brought up in a cultured and musical family. She became a talented pianist, often accompanying her father when he sang at parties and musical evenings at friends' homes. She completed a course at the Triangle Secretarial College in London, then in her early twenties she obtained a job with the Imperial Continental Gas Association.

Socially in the fast lane, she was popular, beautiful and amusing. Her sister Molly wrote that "Nancy dashed about in fast cars". She enjoyed high society, mixing with the London social elite. She was invited to sit for a portrait by Richard Jack, the award-winning portrait painter, and later a prominent war artist for Canada.

The pieces were falling into place. In 1918, Nancy's aunt Stella had married Sir James Stevenson. Sometime before 1924, Sir James had been appointed Chairman of the British Empire Exhibition to sort out serious budgetary problems. To drum up support for the exhibition to be held in 1924/25, there would be a ten-month world tour by various dignitaries, including the famous crime writer Agatha Christie. The tour was dubbed the *Grand Tour*.

Archie Christie's friend, the insufferable, bad-tempered, pompous Major Ernest Belcher, the assistant general manager of the Exhibition, was the tour leader. He appointed Archie as the financial advisor. After ten months away, travelling with his wife Agatha and the delegation to Africa, Australia, New Zealand, Hawaii and Canada, they returned to England. Archie was unable to find a new job and was somewhat unsettled. Their marriage started to fall to pieces.

Nancy was also a friend of Belcher and it was in 1925 that both Nancy and Agatha Christie were invited to work on the same committee. Their job was to plan and create a children's area in the Exhibition. It is probably not a coincidence as Nancy's aunt Stella was married to the chairman of the Exhibition, Sir James Stevenson, and it is very likely that Stella arranged for Nancy to work there.

Around this time a friend from secretarial college invited Nancy to attend a weekend house party at her house near Godalming, south of Windsor. These weekend house parties, a feature of the times, were all about having fun – gossiping, some sport, eating, drinking, dancing and, of course, sex. Nancy often stayed with friends near Windsor for these weekend occasions. It is not hard to imagine her, dressed in a shocking knee length skirt, probably a little under the weather, wildly dancing the Charleston, beads swinging, arms swaying and legs kicking. Archie Christie also attended these weekend parties. He became infatuated by the beautiful sexy young woman, ten years his junior. The affair blossomed.

Archie finally announced to Agatha that he was in love with 'another woman' and demanded a quick divorce. However, after a short separation, he returned. Coming back proved to be a mistake and he announced in early December of 1926 that he had decided to finally leave Agatha to marry Nancy. By then, Nancy had been meeting Archie every weekend. He packed his bags and left for a friend's house — Nancy was waiting.

That same day, December 3rd, Agatha disappeared. Her car was found over an embankment at Newlands Corner in Surrey with the bonnet up and the lights on. Inside were her fur coat, suitcase, and her expired driver's licence. For ten days there was a nationwide search involving over 500 policemen in four counties and 15,000 volunteers. Rumours flew around suggesting suicide, murder, kidnapping.

The police and volunteers dragged rivers and searched forests to no avail. She was eventually found at the Hydropathic Hotel in Harrogate, registered under the name of Mrs Neele of Cape Town. Agatha claimed that the reason for her extraordinary disappearance was loss of memory caused by the emotional stress. The hunt for the real Miss Neele (Archie's lover) was on.

Nancy's sister Molly wrote in her autobiography:

> *Nannie guarded the front door like a bloodhound and only opened it quickly when one of us arrived and [shut it again if she could] before a reporter could get his foot in it. Anonymous letters came by every post. Nancy's uncle, Ivor Fraser, General Manager of the Morning Post and cousin-in-law, Sir Neville Pearson, owner of Country Life magazine, were begged to use their influence to cool things a bit. Mother was in tears, neighbours' curtains twitched, her brothers the twins, Kingston and Anthony and I had to run the gauntlet nightly, returning from work. A reporter put his foot in the door saying, "You are the sister, you must give me the story. My kids will starve if you don't". Eventually I shook him off without a story.*

Six months later Nancy's aunt, Dame Ethel Pearson, took Nancy away on a cruise around the world "to forget", but Nancy was determined. The separation failed to quell the passion. Avril Johnstone, Aunt Stella's adopted daughter, was also taken on the trip in an equally fruitless family attempt to lure her away from her lover, *Simon the Greek,* whom she later married.

~

Agatha and Archie were divorced in April, 1928. For the rest of her long life, despite the fact that they had a daughter Rosalind, Agatha never spoke of Archie nor had any contact with him. Archie has been described in the media as a bounder and a cad, but Agatha was not often criticised for her part in the breakup. However in a 2010 review by Roger Lewis of Richard Hack's book, *Duchess of Death,* he wrote in conclusion "I am left wondering: was Agatha Christie a lesbian? Was a fatal lack of sexual chemistry what made Archie so frustrated and why he had to bolt?"

Archie married Nancy Neele at St. George's Church in Hanover Square, London, in October 1928. They remained married until she died on 13th August, 1958. Archie died on 20th December, 1962. They had one child, a son Archibald, known as "Beau", born in 1930. It will never be known if Archie seduced Nancy or if the beautiful, vivacious Nancy seduced Archie. Perhaps it was for both love at first sight.

Another

George Graves

Does the moon shine as brightly
when no one is staring?
Does the grass grow as greenly
when no one is caring?
Are the oceans as blue
when no one is sailing?

Do the birds sing as sweetly
    when no one is listening?
Do the eyes sparkle as brightly
    when no one is watching?
And are the lips as soft
    when no one is kissing?

The sceptic may say we make no
    difference.
The sun shall rise and the sun shall set
    regardless of man or woman;
    and that is all there is.

And yet;
The awe of the night sky is unknown
    if the child is sleeping,
The wonder of the rainbow is unseen
    if the child is dreaming,
The softness of the sand is unfelt
    if no one is wandering,
And the murmur of the brook is unheard
    if no one is listening.

A person can enjoy all this by themselves.
And yet;
The brilliance of the sunset
and the shimmer on the ocean,
The grandeur of the canyon
and the thunder of the surf,
The sweetness of the berries
and the perfume of the roses;
Everything is enhanced by having a friend
standing beside me,
exploring the wonders of the universe
and the intricacies of the heart,
looking, feeling, listening,
tasting the salt air,
together,
the touch of her fingers on mine.

The Slow Process of Decay

KJ Mair

This is a ghost story. Please don't forget.

~

On a wet Tuesday in June 2012, I died.

For two minutes and twenty-three seconds I was dead. Then somehow I wasn't. I could move. I could breath. I existed again.

I'm still trying to figure out how I feel about that.

~

The dog doesn't like me anymore. She doesn't come near me. She growls when I get too close.

Tom keeps saying I should get rid of her, that I should give the fleabag away. Give it to someone who could actually pat the little beast without getting a mean bite.

But how can I? When Adam had loved the mutt so very much.

I put the dog food in the bowl and back away until I'm half hidden in the doorway. I keep still and silent. The dog takes hesitant steps towards the food. She sniffs with suspicious caution for a moment, and then dives in with animal gusto.

I watch and listen to the crack of dog biscuits being crunched. It sounds a lot like bones snapping.

~

I have my head on Tom's chest. If I listen closely I can hear his heartbeat.

"What do you see when you look at me?" I whisper.

The beat skips and dances as he considers his answer. I wonder at the thoughts that cause every missed step.

"What do you mean?"

Tom has mastered the art of distance. He's the questioner of questions, the dodger of eyes and the whisperer of the barest of touches. He's made a home in the silence of words gone unsaid.

"Never mind," I concede.

I think about absences of the heart, if his ever yearns for mine in his self-imposed exile? I can't speak the fondness of my own. I have a stranger's heart now and I don't know what it wishes.

I reach up and nuzzle into his neck. I kiss his pulse and I feel it jump. I smile secretly. He touches my breast and I let out a pleased moan. His fingers graze my scar, the one that marks the divide between my right and my left, and he hesitates. He shouldn't. He should press in until it hurts.

One of my hands drifts south, hungry with intent.

"Wait."

He grabs my hand and our wedding bands clink. It's a kiss of metal, like the brakes pushed flat against the floor.

I sigh and turn over, not wanting to hear the repeated refrain. I'm tired of his excuses. I'm so tired of waiting.

~

Time doesn't heal. It numbs. I understand how people get it wrong.

I sit in the rain and watch the play-set rust. The swing sways without anyone sitting on it. Water cascades down the slippery dip and I wonder if Adam would have liked water slides.

My bare toes sink into the mud and I feel the wriggling of worms. I encourage them. They have a job to do and they've been lax in their work ethic. We're all destined to be worm food in the end, after all.

~

The lights flicker on and I flinch.

There, staring back at me, with eyes I don't trust, is me.

It's late. So late, I know I won't be disturbed. Tom's loud snores can't be heard from down the hall and even the fleabag has stopped her whiny barking.

I need the quiet to do this. It's something that I have skilfully avoided for a while. I stare at the mirror and with careful fingers I slowly open my shirt, like some sort of masturbatory self-seduction.

With every button pop, more and more of my scar is revealed. It's a deep angry red thing that stretches from my collarbone to the top of my stomach. I trace it with an unsteady finger and my breath hitches at every puckered hill.

Sometimes I wish I could force my fingers between the healed stitches and rip myself open. It would be kinder and more honest than the counterfeit life I'm living.

A stranger's heart is beating in my chest.

Though that's not exactly true. We did have a short meeting on a wet Tuesday afternoon. It's hard to believe I can hate someone so much for only knowing them the briefest of moments. Aren't you supposed to hate those who know you best?

"Who were you?"

Even as I say it, I know it's the wrong question. I should be asking, who *are* you?

I'm too scared of the answer to voice the question out loud. I don't know who will answer back.

What a troubling realisation. I'm haunted by a ghost I can see.

~

I used to love red wine. Now I hate it.

Something about it seems too rich, too flat and far too red. I take a sip and nearly choke on the taste. Quickly I reach out and steal Tom's beer right out of his hand. I brush his fingers and he lets the bottle go easily, hastily. I chug down the beer and for once it's refreshing and pleasant. It's strange, I remember it being the opposite.

"Do you have to drink so much?" Tom rubs his face hard. His palms held tight against his eye socket. "Haven't you learnt yet?"

Other than taking another sip, I ignore him.

We both stare out into the yard where the play-set used to be. We have just finished packing it up. The slide was never used, so it's going to the Salvos where hopefully a happy young family can find some joy from it. However, the swing's chains were far too rusted and are at the bottom of the bin.

All that is left is squashed yellow grass and an obnoxious dog chewing on a stick.

"I want a divorce," Tom says.

I'm not surprised. To be honest I was expecting it sooner.

"Well, I've done the dead part of, *till death do us part.* So I suppose you've fulfilled your contractual obligations."

"Jesus! Can't you take things seriously for once? Look with Adam de—"

"Don't," I snap.

I take another swig of beer and it tastes less satisfying than the first. Tom snatches the beer away and some of the liquid goes flying. It drips down the back steps in a steady beat.

"Look, if you had just talked about it, we wouldn't be in this mess."

"That's the thing though, isn't it? Even if I had talked, even if I shared every fucked up thought inside my head, you would never have heard me." I look into his eyes for what feels like the first time in eons. "You think I'm the one that should have died instead of Ad … instead of him."

I lean up close to Tom, so close that my lips are grazing his ear. "And you know what? You're absolutely right."

I brush a kiss to the tip of his ear and then I walk away.

"Wait," he sputters.

I keep going. It feels good to be the one leaving him waiting for once.

~

I don't know why I'm here. And when she opens the door, I still don't have an answer.

Her eyes are dark and they go even darker when she recognises me. I am more surprised at the spark of recognition that flares inside me. There is part of me that wants to reach up and touch her hair.

What a treacherous heart.

What does she see when she looks at me? Can she give me an answer when my husband gave none?

"You're her, aren't you? You're the one who …"

She looks torn, like she can't decide whether to slap me or invite me in. I can see her eyeing the tip of my scar that's peeking out from under my shirt. I pull up my neckline to cover it.

"He was a good man, you know. My husband."

I was wrong to come here. I turn to leave.

"It wasn't his fault. The crash. It wasn't his fault."

I'm walking and then I'm running. Even still, I can hear her last accusation.

"It was *yours*."

~

I get him flowers. I hope he likes them, daisies for such a sunny boy.

I trace the first A in his name and leave a smear of pollen behind. I'm ashamed that this is my first visit. I hope my little boy forgives me. I certainly won't.

It's been so much easier to have a stranger to blame. To hate. Easier still when there's a piece of him living inside me. All those negative feelings are being pushed inwards anyway, so why not serve up a target?

But this is a ghost I must put to rest.

I admit I drank too much red wine that afternoon. I remember my breath had reeked of it. Adam had scrunched up his little nose. It was easier to take another sip than think of the way Tom would light up for our son and not for me.

Even though I knew it was a risk, I hadn't done the right thing — like wait. Call a taxi. Call Tom. Catch a bus. Anything. Anything. Any one of them.

I had done the dumb, stupid thing instead.

And on a wet Tuesday in June 2012, I paid the price.

I see the weight of it now in the numbers underneath my son's name. In the dash that's too short. Between the numbers that are not far enough apart.

I lie down on his grave and I wonder if he can feel me under six feet of dirt, grit and a guilty heart.

---

* This story was awarded Second Prize in the Alice Sinclair Memorial Writing Competition in 2016, and published in *HPA Magazine*, issue 2 2017.

Under the Sea

Pam Garfoot

Fairy tales are very sad, and often cruel. I discovered this the day after my eighth birthday. Hans Christian Andersen was to blame.

It was past bedtime and my sister's regular breathing from the bunk below mine told me she was sleeping. I couldn't wait to read *Fairy tales retold for little children*. Its green cover was shiny, new and full of promise. Depicted on it was a kind-faced man sitting on a stool telling stories to a group of cross-legged, smiling children dressed in dirndl dresses and folk caps. Beside them on the grass a small rabbit listened too.

There were three stories in my book, each a little more disturbing than the last. I read first of the emperor and his new clothes. How funny it was to see the vain emperor sauntering amongst his subjects wearing long red underwear. The story of tiny Thumbelina also pleased me, but something dark and brooding was creeping in. Thumbelina was so diminutive that she slept in a walnut shell. She revived a frozen swallow which was close to death, then flew away on his back. By the story's end Thumbelina had married the equally tiny king of the flower angels. I was distraught to see the picture of the frozen swallow, but rejoiced at the happy ending.

The book's last and most troubling story told of the little mermaid. I read of the youngest mermaid princess who fell in love with a shipwrecked prince. She rescued him and left him on the shore near his family castle. So great was her love for him that she sacrificed her beautiful voice to the sea witch so that, in exchange, her mermaid tail could be replaced by little white legs. The mermaid wanted to become human and to offer her silent love to the prince at his castle. Here the story took a sorrowful turn. The mermaid was never able to speak of how she had saved the prince from the shipwreck or tell him of her love. He broke her heart by falling in love with a princess from another land. After dancing all night on her tender new legs at the wedding of the princess and prince, the mermaid flung herself into the sea and disappeared forever into the churning waves.

I cried so to think of the mermaid having tried to turn herself into something she could never be, all for a doomed love. I closed my little green-covered book and knew that I was different now. My innocence was forever gone.

~

I grew up with my three siblings by the sea, in a small town on the south coast. Our house lay next to a deep, slow-flowing creek that meandered down to the ocean. The creek was our playground and a motley group of old canoes was permanently pulled up in our backyard, ready for adventure. When not exploring the creek, or reading on my bed, I would be in the ocean swimming and playing. I often imagined mermaid friends when I dived beneath the foamy waves.

Although I was happy in my seaside playground, at school I was shy and solitary. I had few friends, especially at the high school which I attended in a nearby town. However, when I was in my final year at the school a new young man came to class. His fair hair was loose with curls and his demeanour was quiet, but strong. I determined to be his friend. He told me he aspired to study at a university in a large inland city and later, when we both applied for the same university, I knew our fate was sealed.

Throughout the next year, as we began our studies, my love for the young man grew. Yet I never spoke of it to him, always hoping he would realise that he felt the same love for me. Gradually our studies meant that we spent less time together. He had his classes, and I had mine.

Nonetheless, on Thursday afternoons we had a habit of walking together from our residential halls to the one lecture our courses shared. We would take a winding bushy path and often stayed silent, content it seemed in each other's company.

One Thursday, well into autumn, the weather was unseasonably mild. We sprawled on the lawns outside the lecture hall waiting for four o'clock to roll around. There was a pleasant warmth in the sun and only the lightest of breezes. All was so peaceful we could almost hear the golden leaves falling to the soft grass.

"What do you long for?" I asked him, as I idly arranged leaves in a pattern across the carpet of green.

The young man plucked at the grass distractedly. He was surprised by my question. But at last he spoke.

"I don't know … maybe I long for a great love. Someone to share my thoughts with."

I looked across at his flushed face, and then playfully leant across to push him over.

"Oh, you have me, don't you?" I said, and we laughed a little.

A group of other students then flowed into the courtyard and walked across towards the lecture hall. The young man's head turned towards them. From the periphery of my vision, I could see his eyes follow a tallish and beautifully slender girl with hair that glowed auburn in the late afternoon sunlight. Nothing further was said between us. We rose, brushed the grass and leaves from our clothes and followed the group into the darkened hall.

Not long after this, I dyed my mousey hair a reddish honey colour. I took to skipping meals in the communal dining room. When I saw the young man again he did not notice my hair.

"You're pale," he said. "You don't look well. Perhaps you are pushing yourself too hard on those essays."

I kicked at some gravel and pulled my jacket in against the chill, saying nothing. Still, the next Thursday we walked again together along the bush path towards our lecture, and shared a long discussion about Shakespearean plays.

As we approached the lecture hall the auburn-haired girl appeared. The young man veered away to join her. I stopped then to watch as they stood close, sharing a quiet conversation. I felt weak and dizzy, and it seemed as if my heart had stopped beating. Other students were wending their way, singly and in groups, into the hall but my leaden legs would not move me. I stood a solitary figure outside in the wind. Then, with a burst of clarity, I swung around and walked back to my dim and cheerless room.

Some weeks later, the mid-year recess saw many students return to their homes for a week's break. I would rather have curled up under my bed covers and shunned the light for the entire week, but my mother rang to make sure I had booked my bus fare home. She and my father were happily planning some home-style care and attention, and my siblings were looking forward to my return. I could not say no.

The following afternoon, I stepped down from the bus on to the footpath in the centre of my little home town. My mother had been eagerly awaiting my arrival. I could see her head bobbing excitedly up and down as she scanned all the passengers for my familiar face. Her smile vanished as she caught sight of me, but she pulled me into a long hug and steered me across to the car.

Later, in the fading evening light, I went down to the creek and pulled a canoe into the water. I pushed out into the creek with the oars, then aimlessly floated there. The canoe drifted slowly on the turning tide. The water's surface was a black mirror to the brooding sky and a scattering of tiny flying insects pocked the dark surface. After a time, a decision came to me. I would contact the young man, for he too would be home for the break, and tell him my feelings if I could. I suspected the auburn-haired girl had come here too, but I would find a way to speak my mind.

Two days later the three of us walked along the wide, firm sand at the beach. There was a winter crispness in the air and a brisk wind blew, whisking our words away as we spoke them. After we had been walking a little while I turned to the others to speak, and saw their hands entwined. He was looking down at her and brushing her auburn hair, wild with wind, from her face with a tenderness that twisted a knife inside me. Something within was mortally wounded, and a desperate coldness crept towards my heart. Yet I turned towards the sea again and remained silent, closing my eyes tight against the tears.

In time we came to an inlet, where an old weathered jetty extended out into a wide expanse of deep and choppy water. Further up the slope which rose from the inlet was a cluster of houses and one or two shops, but no other walkers braved the chilly wind. My chance had come.

I needed coffee, I said. Perhaps someone could walk up to the small store and purchase three coffees for us? Soon the two of us were alone.

~

It is clear to me now that the young man will never love me. I walk back and forth along the jetty. My hands shake and my breaths are short. Stepping close behind the auburn-haired girl I know what I must do. Only moments remain.

Soon I have completed half my plan. In time I see a figure walking down the slope, carrying a cardboard tray of warm drinks. It is time for me to disappear under the surface one final time. I will dissolve now into the foamy water. My reddish honey hair will be carried on the tide along with her auburn hair. We two will forever mingle in the arms of the ocean.

The figure treads carefully down to the jetty then pauses, scanning the scene for our familiar silhouettes. Soon the young man will rush in confusion along the heavy grey planks and wonder where the two of us have gone.

———

The Moon in the Pond

Tony Lang

The story I'm about to tell
Took place a while ago,
A year or maybe more — Oh well,
A hundred years or so.

I'm starting to get old these days –
Be patient if you would!
I see, as in the past I gaze
A green and pleasant wood.

A pond is in a clearing there
Where dreamy waters deep
Shelter fish and frogs and where
The moon comes down to sleep.

At least that's what we creatures thought
Once upon a time.
But some an explanation sought
And so you have this rhyme.

When the moon was full and round
And night was bright as day
We that live upon the ground
Came out to romp and play.

But weariness would come too soon,
We'd pause, a drink to take,
And that is when we'd see the moon
On the bottom of the lake.

How could she be so far away
And in the pond below?
Although we pondered night and day
We did not really know.

The answer came one moonlit night
Upon a gentle breeze.
The moon had listened to our plight
And answered all our pleas:

"Each night I did this earth traverse,
Looking down, serene,
I longed to see the universe
That I had never seen.

One night I looked into the pond —
Saw my reflected face,
And then I saw what lay beyond —
My family in space!

I saw the stars — the twinkling ones
That hung in bright festoons;
I saw a million, million suns,
A million, million moons.

So when you look into the pond
You'll see my shining face,
Looking to the stars beyond,
To my family in space."

Now when we creatures of the wood
Come out to romp and play,
What once we never understood
Is now as clear as day.

One moon watches us and smiles
To see us at our play;
The other looks across the miles
At her family, far away.

---

* This poem was published in *HPA Magazine,* issue 5 2018.

Calming the Storm

Cate Plink

Carol woke just as the early morning light was seeping through the wooden slats of the blinds. She opened her eyes, groaned and closed them again. When oh when was she going to learn how to sleep past five-thirty? Sam seemed to have no trouble adjusting his pattern. Why couldn't she?

A few months ago, Sam had taken early retirement, and she, a little reluctantly, had followed suit. They had taken a long tour of Europe and North America. It had been incredibly exciting, and Carol had loved it. Sam seemed to have enjoyed it as well in his own quiet way. That was how it had always been with them, Sam's quiet nature offsetting her own stormier soul. Her mother had once told her that she and Sam were a perfect partnership, and she believed it.

Just lately though, it seemed as if that partnership wasn't working the same anymore. Since their return from the trip she'd found Sam's quiet acceptance of their retirement lifestyle frustrating her, rather than calming her. Didn't he realise how many times a day she wanted to rage against the quietness of retirement life? He would happily sit in the garden with his easel, painting the flowerbeds, the trees, the sky. Other days he joined the walking group, taking pictures along the way to turn into even more paintings.

Carol wasn't keen on walking, so rarely went along, and her only hobbies were knitting and sewing. Now their grandchildren were all well into their teens, there was nobody really to sew or knit for, which only left a weekly outing to Bingo, which she wasn't all that enthused about either.

As usual sleep wouldn't come back, so Carol finally got up and went through to the kitchen to make herself a cup of tea. As she sat sipping it, she thought about the day ahead. A quick sweep and vacuum the floors. Run a duster around the lounge. A few breakfast dishes to do and the bed to make. Not enough washing for a load, so what next? It wasn't a Bingo day, so it looked as if it would be just another day at home, reading, knitting or fiddling about on the internet. If she couldn't find a way to change her life, she was going to expire from pure boredom.

It was seven-thirty when Sam came into the kitchen, by which time she had finished the dusting, done the vacuuming and was washing the shining-clean windows in the kitchen. Sam gently removed the cloth and the cleaning spray from her hand.

"You did those two days ago, sweetheart," he told her. "You've already done the lounge, bathroom, and bedroom windows this week too."

Carol sat down at the table and looked at Sam hopelessly. The tears she'd been holding back, finally overflowed.

"Is this it, Sam? Is this our life from now on? It's alright for you. You have your painting, and that seems to be enough for you. But what have I got? Bingo, knitting or sewing, talking to almost complete strangers on the internet. I'm going crazy Sam, crazy." Her voice rose hysterically.

Sam put his arms around her and held her close.

"We'll think of something, sweetheart," he told her. "I have an idea for today anyway."

"We weeded the garden yesterday." Carol sighed.

"I know, but how about I take you out for lunch? We haven't had a day away for a long time. We can drive up the coast, and maybe stay overnight somewhere."

Once again Sam had come up with the perfect way to calm the storm within her.

"Oh yes, wonderful," she gave him a huge hug and flew down the hall to prepare.

~

Sam watched his wife hurry up the hall. She was happy for now, but for how long? He hoped the idea he had would work out. He'd made enough to make sure that they had a good life with a wonderful home, trips overseas, and expensive jewellery for Carol.

However, he'd always craved the quieter life of retirement, hating the hustle and bustle of the corporate world he'd worked in.

Carol had worked because she wanted to, not because they needed her income. She had fretted when not occupied. Once the children were old enough, she'd pleaded to do at least part-time work. Sam had understood her desire to be busy and had not said anything against it. Now was different. Until a week ago, Sam had worried deeply about Carol's inability to accept her retirement. *Maybe,* he thought to himself, *retiring at sixty hadn't been such a great idea after all.* Then he'd seen something online, just by chance and the idea had blossomed.

~

Carol loved the drive up the coast. Sam took as many backroads as he could, often travelling along the shore. Carol sat looking out the window, loving the peaceful feeling of the small towns along the way. Maybe if they lived up here, the beauty of the surroundings would somehow soothe her stormy mind.

They stopped for lunch in an attractive village, eating *al-fresco* style overlooking the bay with the boats bobbing peacefully at anchor. Afterwards as they continued along the coast, Carol couldn't help feeling the serenity of the view seeping deep into her soul.

"It's lovely, isn't it?" Sam remarked once.

"Oh, it is. It's just wonderful. Thanks for today, I've enjoyed it so much."

"I'm glad you feel better. I'd hoped you'd like being up here." Sam patted her hand gently.

Carol noticed that lights were coming on in the little townships they were passing. "Where are we staying?" She asked after a while. "It's getting late."

"Just down there," Sam replied. Carol looked where he was pointing and saw a small group of lights, and the moon shining on the bay.

"Oh, how beautiful," she sighed.

She was silent as they drove down the hill to the township. Somehow the beauty of the sight did not need conversation.

~

Sam was also silent during the approach to the town. His mind was filled with childhood memories of this place. Wonderful summer days running free with a multitude of cousins. Other, cooler days fishing or sailing on the lake with his father and grandfather. Warm evenings sitting on the porch watching the moonlight on the water and dreaming the dreams of a child. He'd missed this place more than he thought he had.

He drove through the main street past the cluster of shops — more than he remembered — and past the small hotel, then turned to follow the waterfront for a short distance. He pulled up outside a large green guesthouse. He was surprised to note that what had once been a grassy common ground, used by campers in the summer, had become a large permanent holiday park. That augured well for his plans he thought to himself.

"Come on," he said to Carol, "this is where we are staying."

"Oh, it's so quaint, I love it." She smiled at him in delight.

An elderly man sat behind the counter of the reception desk. He glanced at the name as they registered, then looked harder at Sam, who grinned at him.

The man laughed. "Sam Rivers! You're Frank's grandson. I remember what a bunch of tearaways you and all those cousins of yours were."

"That's right, Tom. Do you remember teaching me to row in that creaky old dinghy of yours?"

"Oh yes, I did too. You tipped us over one time. Bloody cold it was too. Long time ago now," the old man sighed a little sadly. "You won't find many of my lot left these days."

"I don't expect so, Tom. I'll have a long chat with you about those days, and cold dips in the lake." He grinned at Tom. "Right now, I'd better get settled in. Is there a table for dinner?"

"Sure is. I'll let the cook know. She'll be happy to see you too. It's Mary Sommers. Do you remember her? We've been married forty-five years this year."

"I thought you had a thing for her back in the day, Tom. Can the two of you join us after you've finished with dinner?"

Sam could feel his wife's eyes on him as they went upstairs to the room Tom had allocated them.

"I'll just pop down and park the car," he said quickly before she had time to say anything. He hoped she wouldn't be too angry about his hidden agenda for the day, but he could tell she did like the place, which was a great start.

~

Carol's mind was in turmoil as she waited for Sam to get back. She should have known that he had something up his sleeve. He often did. Sam was deep, very deep. Still in all their married years he hadn't disappointed with his surprises. Her sixtieth birthday had been the fabulous cruise, and last Christmas had been perfect. She hoped that this plan would turn out as well.

She walked over to the window and looked out. It was such a beautiful sight. The bay was very still with the lights from the towns on the other side twinkling on the water, and the full moon casting a moon-glade wide enough to dance on. For the first time in months she felt her spirits lift.

She was still there when Sam came back from parking the car. He crossed the room and put his arms around her, dropping a kiss on the top of her head. She turned in his arms and looked up into his smiling face.

"You, my devious husband, are up to something aren't you?"

"Well, yes I am." He kissed her quickly. "Do you think you can wait until dinner for the answer? I don't think you're going to be disappointed."

"Do I have to?"

"Yes." He laughed and kissed her again. "Get changed into something nice, and let's go down to dinner."

Carol enjoyed the meal. It wasn't *haute cuisine,* but it was well cooked and tasty. The room was fairly full, and everybody seemed to be having fun. They were just finishing their dessert, when Tom and his wife came and sat down with them. Tom produced a bottle of wine and poured for them. Carol liked Tom's wife, Mary, and they chatted together for a while. Finally, though, her curiosity would not be contained.

"Okay Sam, I think I would like to be told what this is all about." She looked inquiringly at her husband.

~

Sam sat for a moment or two, this was it, make or break time. He just hoped she liked the idea. It was vital to him that she did. Ever since he'd seen that piece online, he'd known what he wanted to do. This was where he wanted to stay forever, back where he'd been happier than any other time in his life.

"Carol," he started, "Tom and Mary are selling this place, and I want to buy it. We would live here, next to the water. It's busy in the summer, and the school holidays, but it's closed in winter so then we'd be able to have wonderful holidays. You'd be busy most of the time, I know, but that's what you want, isn't it?"

He looked anxiously at his wife. She was smiling all over her face.

"Oh Sam, what a wonderful idea. I'd never be bored again."

"It's a lot of work, Carol," Mary told her.

"I don't mind work. It's not having enough to do that drives me crazy."

Sam watched Carol talking animatedly to Mary. He'd done it again, calmed the storm within his wife. Now perhaps he could find the time to truly enjoy the retirement he'd worked so hard for.

Ode to Pushka

Elizabeth Horwitz

Cat power extended,
graciously and gracefully
a royal movement as she came
to lick the offered milk
then she retreated to the bush.
A dignified old lady yet agile and alert
as strays are …

Closer she came, and I started
the ritual all over again.
Foil containers of cat food,
offers of bedding
as she took up a shaky residence.
Pretty, appealing and aloof
until she chose to sleep inside.

The shriek of the great storm
and the clatter of helmeted men
made her flee … then
timidly accept.
Was she battered in the past?
This old yet new creature
I could now call mine
as much as she would let me.

She was sent to be with me
I believe,
in a year of uncertainty and
new, sometimes frightening, events.
She sheltered me, as I gave
her shelter, a companion-like love
and mutual understanding.

A princess of the ancient past
was she choosing me
to make her closing years comfortable?
Hospitality and acceptance of this
takes many forms …
Thank you, my elegant beloved old cat,
for spending lost time
and love with me.

Glitter and Grit

Alison Ferguson

In the shade of the scrubby trees, my picnic blanket provided little protection from the stony ground. To sit on the beach by the glittering lake would have been more comfortable, but the sun was too fierce. Levering another cushion under me, I perched with my legs stretched out. I squinted against the sun, which had begun its steady westward descent. The lake's surface rippled in ribbons of molten gold, disturbed by the bathers splashing knee-deep by the shore. From my vantage point, I could watch them without being seen. Their shouts of laughter reached me easily across the narrow sandy strip.

Someone called out, "Come on, Jane. If you're going to marry Henry, it's high time you learned to swim."

Jane took a step back, as if frightened they'd pull her in. Every inch the country girl, her hair plaited and pinned, she'd probably never been in water deeper than her ankles. I should have felt sorry for her, I supposed. Henry came to her side, taking the opportunity to slide his arm around her. I was glad to see he kept his hand decorously in the small of her back. He was saying something to her so quietly that I couldn't hear it.

"Watch yourself, Henry," called his friend, walking backward into the deeper water. "An officer can't be seen to be improper. You don't see Rose and me whispering sweet nothings."

"Don't be a tease, Jack," laughed Rose. "Just because we've been engaged forever. And besides, the way you flirt, the war will be over before you're made an officer." She skidded the palm of her hand across the water, drenching him.

Good on her, I thought. Nothing of the silly timid goose about her.

"Right, if that's how you want it," Jack dived to the deeper water, staying submerged until he came back around to rise up tossing water with both hands.

Within seconds, Henry had joined them and their fight took them out into the darker water where their wet heads bobbed up and down like seals.

Only Jane stayed apart, still standing in the shallows, a frozen smile fixed to her face. Her hands were clasped, her fingers working nervously. The diamond ring on her left hand glinted intermittently as if sending Morse code — an SOS, perhaps.

Amid much splashing, the others were back. Jack launched himself on Henry and they wrestled on the wet sand like puppies.

Rose, gasping with laughter, took Jane's hand. "Come on. We'd better get out of their way. Once these two get started, there's no stopping them."

Rose dragged her out into the lake. As the water reached their waists, Jane baulked, just as I knew she would. She tugged her hand away. With both arms stretched out for balance, it looked like her feet were fighting for purchase as the shelf of sand dropped away sharply.

Behind them, the young men rolled on their backs in the shallow water, their chests heaving, covered in gritty sand.

"Got you!" shouted Jack, and he lunged forward toward Rose, jetting along the surface on his stomach.

Jane shrieked as his bow wave swamped her too. She dog-paddled for the shore, holding her chin high, trying to keep her head out of the water.

There, I knew you could swim if you had to, girlie. I chuckled at the contrast — Rose gleefully dunking Jack's head under the water, and Jane's eyes fixed on Henry who was still sitting in the shallows. He was going to have trouble keeping his two friends if he married such a ninny.

I closed my eyes against the glare of the westering sun. From the far distant shore, I could catch the drone of the Catalina sea-planes as they began to return to base.

"That's my girl," encouraged Henry. "You're nearly there."

By the sound of it, Jack and Rose had splashed their way to shore.

"Rose and I are going up to the point to see the pelicans," Jack said. "Coming you two?"

I shaded my eyes to see what was going on.

Henry had gone several steps before checking over his shoulder for Jane. She was still sitting in the shallows, her hands sunk into the sand on either side of her.

"Jane?"

"No, no. You go. I'll stay in the water for a bit longer."

Now I was fully awake. Why would she want to stay in the water? Bored with the antics of Jack and Rose? Well, maybe — their high spirits wouldn't be everyone's cup of tea. But, why stay in the water that she so obviously feared?

"That's an idea," Henry said. "Get some practice in without these blighters getting in the way. We won't be long." He gave her a cheerful wave and pounded along the sand to catch up to the others.

Jane stayed where she was, watching their retreating backs.

Slowly her hands emerged and she stared intently at them, turning them this way and that.

Had she been stung by something? Then I realised what was missing — not even a glimmer. She'd lost her engagement ring.

Stupid, foolish girl. Did the engagement mean so little to her?

She looked toward where Henry had gone with his friends.

She should call out but, by the look of it, she wasn't going to call for help. But this wasn't something you could hide — a man liked to see the ring he'd spent his savings on. Mind you, he'd be angry. Did she fear him? This was no way to start a marriage.

Her hands began to move across the surface of the water, as if trying to clear away the sheen so that she could see the broken shells below. Abandoning caution, she thrust her hands through the water down deep into the sand, bringing up handful after handful of grit that cascaded between her fingers.

She looked toward the others. She was going to call.

Good, she couldn't do this alone. She was the sort that always needed help. Poor Henry was going to find her a heavy burden. Perhaps this would be the final straw? It was only an engagement, after all.

As if on cue, the others turned to wave but all she did was wave back. She turned to stare across the lake. She crossed her arms tightly in front of her stomach as she curled up. I thought I heard a low moan.

I could help, I supposed, though I'm old now and my sight isn't quite what it was. Did she know I was watching? The girl knew she was out of her depth, marrying an officer and moving from the country. Somewhere inside herself she wanted to get out of the engagement and this was her chance.

Abruptly, she stood up, staring intently across the lake, as if getting her bearings. She bent over and began to walk about in the shallows, each step purposeful. She straightened, looked out again, then resumed her search. She was retracing her steps.

So, not as silly as she seemed.

The water was deeper now, and she still hadn't found it. When it was lapping at her waist, she paused, both elbows held high as if resting on the air above. She swayed oddly, as if moving her feet about through the sand and lake weed, relying on her toes to feel for the ring.

She'd be too frightened to go any further. One more step and she'd be off the warm sandy shelf and into the dark cold water. Once there, she'd have to dive to search the lake bed. It took courage to do something for which you were so ill-prepared. Would she dive?

The shouts of the others drifted on the easterly breeze as they began to walk back. They'd spotted Jane now up to her neck in the water and were whooping their encouragement.

She was only going to get one chance at this, I realised. If she dived now, and if she found it, no one ever need know she'd lost it. If she didn't, then the ring wouldn't be the only thing lost. How would Henry react if he knew she had feared to call him — two kinds of trust, both missing in their fragile relationship?

Jane's shoulders heaved as she took a deep breath. She dived.

Involuntarily, I found that I was holding my breath too.

More shouts and clapping echoed down the empty beach as the others saw her take the plunge.

The seconds went by and all I could see on the surface were rippling bubbles.

The others' shouts died. Henry began to run.

Jane's head burst through the surface, her dripping hair in her eyes.

I breathed again.

Her hands were still under the water as she did her awkward dog-paddle toward Henry.

Had she got it? What would my son do if she didn't?

I saw him, swimming alongside her. His relief and pride at his wife-to-be's achievement were written across his face.

And I realised that I desperately wanted her to have found the ring. Underneath her shy surface was exactly the wife that my boy Henry needed — an independent woman who had the courage to face whatever marriage brought.

They reached the shallows, and Jane crouched as if getting a foothold before standing. Her hands came together under the water and then she stood. She waved to where I sat in the shade on the picnic blanket.

The ring on her finger sparkled in the last rays of the setting sun.

The First Line of Defence

James Horn

There are many brave men fighting in New Guinea, and everyday acts of gallantry pass almost unnoticed. One of the bravest men is a brigade liaison officer, who has become a legend with the men. Every day he set out looking for information, equipped with two revolvers, two bandoliers, a sniping rifle, a pocketful of grenades, and a stick in each hand. With this armoury he bagged a Japanese soldier a day … (George H. Johnston New Guinea Diary, 1943)

In the bush on the ridge above my house at Wangi Wangi, New South Wales, there is a concrete bunker, an ammunition dump and four anti-aircraft gun emplacements where the guns have been removed. During the Second World War the guns were placed there to help protect the nearby Rathmines RAAF flying boat base set up just before the war. By 1943 it maintained 14 Catalinas, two Seagulls, a Dornier and a Dolphin. These flying boats based on Lake Macquarie were ideally placed to help defend Australia from Japanese attack. Catalinas were the only RAAF aircraft in service during WWII for the whole of the period of wartime operations against the Japanese. Had it not been for the support provided by the Catalina flying boats tracking the Japanese fleet, the battle of the Coral Sea may have ended very differently. It might have resulted in total destruction of the U.S. Fleet or the sea battle might not have occurred at all. Port Moresby would have been taken by amphibious landing.

After Singapore fell to the Japanese in February 1942, Australians were fearful that the Japanese would invade the Australian mainland. Despite that, Australia was ill-prepared to counter such an attack. The Japanese originally intended to capture Port Moresby, the capital of Australia's colony of Papua New Guinea, by amphibious invasion. In May 1942, the Japanese fleet was en route to Port Moresby but the U.S. fleet had received intelligence warning them. After the Japanese ships were discovered, the Catalina flying boats from Rathmines were ordered to fly there to track their movements and report to U.S. command. Thus, the Japanese fleet was intercepted in the Coral Sea. The seaborne invasion was thwarted, though at horrific cost: ten ships sunk and nearly 1,700 deaths.

On the 21st July 1942, the Japanese forces landed near Buna on the north east side of New Guinea. Their intention was to march across New Guinea using the Kokoda Track, over the Owen Stanley Ranges to attack Port Moresby. The four platoons of the Australian 39th Battalion were unable to hold them back. The track was the overland mail route and comprised a main trail with many parallel and interlocking paths along its length. It rises through dense jungle to heights of 5,000 metres and down to rivers and streams many times. The climate varies from freezing mountain tops to very hot and humid valleys, all with high rainfall. The Kokoda Track was the first line of defence against the only foreign power that had considered an invasion of Australia since the British invasion of 1788.

Anybody who went into the jungle risked being affected by tropical diseases such as malaria, dengue fever, typhus ulcers, dysentery and fungal diseases quite apart from the risks of being fatally bitten by a death adder or taipan snake. Then there were diseases caused by poor food rations and contaminated water; diarrhoea was very common. This is what the Japanese and Australian soldiers faced, of course in addition to the fear of being bayoneted, shot or blown to pieces by hand grenades and bombs.

What follows is my account of my uncle, Captain Burnham C. Fraser's service as a brigade liaison officer attached to the 2/2 Pioneer Battalion, 21st Division of the Australian Infantry Brigade. He fought against the Japanese on the Kokoda Track.

~

On the 7th August 1942, Burnham departed Brisbane for New Guinea. He fought on the Kokoda Track for only ten weeks from 16th August 1942, to 31st October 1942. All along the Track the Australian forces were pushed back. The battalion, having recently fought in the desert in the Middle East, was distinctly disadvantaged. Their uniforms were bleached white from the sun in contrast to the Japanese wearing appropriate dark green uniforms suited to jungle warfare. From the 6th to 8th September, in the Battle of Mission Ridge, the 21st Brigade were almost captured.

In 1973, when pressed by a reporter from *The Age* in Melbourne, Burnham said that he had never talked about the traumas of the Kokoda Track. He then said:

> *I was sitting on the side of a hill, on the top of the Kokoda Track, with two army signallers alongside me and I was counting the Japs as they walked by. The signallers were phoning the numbers back to the brigade: [Burnham said] "I'm sick of counting these blokes." They replied "There's enough anyway." I walked up the Track and a shell from the mountain gun, which had been potting us, landed just where I had been and blew those two coves to smithereens.*

His experiences were also described by Raymond Paull in his book, *Retreat from Kokoda (1958)*:

> *Taking Corporal Beverage, of the Brigade Transport Platoon, Cairns crossed the clearing. The two men had passed Gill's post on the knoll; and were approaching the north-western corner when Beverage said quietly, "Look there's a Jap now." "Give him a grenade" Cairns replied. At the same time he saw the Japanese in the shadows, his light machine-gun aimed at them and his finger curled around the trigger. He called, "Look out", and cast himself flat on the grass, escaping the*

> *burst of fire which echoed his words. The grenade had left Beverage's fingers when the same burst crumpled him. In the next instant, the grenade killed the enemy and destroyed his gun.*
>
> *Cairns, his rifle out of reach, backed away without guessing that Beverage was mortally wounded. Then realising that the corporal had been hit, he circled, saw his body, and returned to retrieve it. His outstretched hand was barely its own breadth from Beverage's ankle when a Japanese leapt from the scrub and charged down upon him. Cairns scrambled to his feet and ran, somewhat blindly, until a deafening roar startled him and he beheld Burnham Fraser, his fellow liaison officer, armed with the cherished marksman's rifle which invariably accompanied him. "Couldn't miss him," said Fraser triumphantly.*

Throughout that morning, Brigade Headquarters' soldiers were engaged in steady fire with the Japanese at the jungle's edge.

Due to his experience as a liaison officer reporting vital information to various Australian commanders along the Kokoda Track and his mapping ability, Burnham was asked to assist the air force supply planes. Knowledge of the mountainous terrain was essential to locate the exact position of the Battalions needing supplies. He not only guided the transport planes, but also instructed pilots and crews how to carry out a supply drop. He was responsible for many successful drops. The planes were comically nicknamed *Biscuit Bombers* because they often parachuted biscuit food rations to the troops.

By then tropical diseases, physical hardship and stress had affected Burnham's health, and he was evacuated to hospital in Port Moresby. The following day he learned that a difficult, dangerous and very important airdrop was to be made at Alola, a signal station about 15 kilometres south of Kokoda, about half way across the Owen Stanley ranges. He realised that his special local knowledge would be invaluable to the Air Force. He was persistent in his request that the Medical Officer release him for the day. It was reported that his cheerful determination and calm guidance ensured a successful mission.

The Japanese advanced to a point within sight of Port Moresby, only a few hundred kilometres from Australia but, unlike the Australian Army, they had outrun their supply lines. They were forced to retreat with the Australians in hot pursuit.

Burnham's war record states the following:

> *Captain Fraser was Liaison Officer attached to 21st Australian Infantry Brigade from 16th August 1942, to 12th September 1942, and during this period displayed exceptional courage and ability in contacting units in difficult positions, often in the face of enemy fire. The extremely difficult terrain, unusual situations and climatic conditions rendered this work particularly enervating and dangerous, but Captain Fraser at no time spared himself.*

Because of ill health diagnosed as peripheral neuritis (beriberi), on the 15th November 1942 he was evacuated back to Australia in a hospital ship and later to Ballarat. The peripheral neuritis resulted from damage to his peripheral nerves. This often causes weakness, numbness and pain in hands and feet. Beriberi is a nervous system ailment resulting from a deficiency of thiamine (vitamin B1). In Burnham's case it was caused by the long period of isolation as a liaison officer at Kokoda. To his dismay, he was required to relinquish his appointment as Liaison Officer. He wrote to his sister Eila in a letter dated 5th November 1942, from Camp 102 A.G.H. Tamworth NSW:

> *... sorting myself out — it was a bit of a jar being pulled out while the show was only half completed. The Doctors were rather in a fog as to what it was ... however they think it's beriberi ... I really have had a wonderful war and heaps of experience, if I could only write short stories.*

Many soldiers returned from the war with serious psychological damage. Was Burnham's comment to Eila his way of putting up a strong front by downplaying the horrors and glorifying the experience? On the 30th January 1943, he again wrote to Eila that he was pleased to receive a letter from their mother, and "on my release [from hospital] last night" he reflected that "hospitals are wretched places." Despite all that he had endured he wrote in the letter: "I'll know this weekend if they will let me go back to active service or not."

On the 21st September 1943 he was examined by the Army Medical Board. They determined that Burnham was suffering from "nervous instability with anxiety". After recuperating he was posted to Victoria Barracks headquarters in Sydney and removed from the active service list as a liaison officer on the 30th October 1943.

As a result of his service during the campaign in the Owen Stanley Ranges, New Guinea during

August to October 1942, it was announced in December 1943 that Burnham had been awarded the Military Cross.

On the 29th December 1943 he was discharged from the army due to beriberi and other physical illnesses from which he suffered for the rest of his life. The medical determination that he was suffering from "nervous instability with anxiety" was never discussed in the family. His daughter-in-law suggested many years later that post-traumatic stress disorder (PTSD) was the reason for his alcoholism. He could never stand hearing babies crying and this was thought to have been due to his terrible war experiences. The symptoms of PTSD are many: substance abuse, anxiety or depression, irritability, avoidance, anger, re-experiencing intrusive memories, images or perceptions, flashbacks, nightmares, exaggerated emotions and physical reactions, avoidance and emotional numbness. Was the alcohol taken by Burnham to deaden the horrors of war or to deaden the pain of his war injuries?

Burnham's cousin twice removed, Justine Hardy, who works in the area of mental health, said in an interview:

> *The mental damage caused by the war has been given many different names over time. More than 2,500 years ago the Greek historian Herodotus described an Athenian warrior "struck down without*

> *blow of sword or dart" as he fell dead in front of Herodotus in the middle of a battle. During the First World War, it was termed "shell shock" and then "battle fatigue", "combat exhaustion" and "war stress" in the Second World War. Now it has a more generic name, post-traumatic stress disorder.*

After the war and his time in hospital recovering from beriberi and the terrible mental torture that he suffered, he returned home to his farm and the calming influence of his wife, Ora. He could not settle back into normal life. They decided to get away from it all and go to *Little 3 Paddock,* over the other side of the plateau from the main homestead. They camped in the bush almost totally isolated from the world for nearly a year. Together they built a log cabin.

General Douglas MacArthur said in 1962:

> *The soldier above all other people prays for peace, for he must suffer and bear the deepest wounds and scars of war.*

Lest we forget

My Sacred Ground

Elizabeth Horwitz

I do not have red poppies in my yard today
yet in a part of my unkempt
garden there are flashes of
a strong orange, centred in black
or purple
self-sown nasturtiums flourishing
boldly and happily each spring.

They make me both sad and
happy as I remember
November of the war to end
all wars. The 11th day of the
11th month — wise words but
wishful thinking.

Have we not learnt, in the agony
of many millenniums of war
often started as a miniature
flash flame of small anger?
Still down your tumbled feelings
and watch and inhale the sweetness of the
flowers in the garden
of your mind.

---

* This poem was published in *HPA Magazine,* issue 5, 2018.

A Whale of a Tale

Jan Mitchell

Whale sharks migrate north along the West Australian coast every winter. They swim quite slowly and now that they are an endangered species, researchers are trying to discover more about them. The research is supported by information and money from the tourist industry — people like me who want to swim with them.

I was swimming as fast as I could with just the top of my snorkel above the water. I was about five metres from the monstrous fish. This one was almost an adult, a male over twenty-five years old and it was as big as a hump-back whale. It was ten metres long, could live for a hundred years and grow another two and a half metres. It was awesome to be swimming alongside one of the biggest fish to have ever existed.

This one wasn't chasing me — not at that stage. I was swimming with my head turned, watching it through my mask and staying aft of its pectoral fins as we'd been instructed. I was bursting with excitement! I could see its pale blue spotted body so clearly; the water conditions were perfect. This was a dream come true, my big Ningaloo Reef adventure in Western Australia just as I had planned it.

Slowly, I fell behind. I finned harder to speed up, trying not to lose sight of the last of the monster whale sharks I had driven 6,000 kilometres to see.

Then something startling happened.

The whale shark turned its head and looked at me. Its eyes seemed as big as dinner plates. The mouth was a wide, grim slit. Wow!

But the fish didn't turn its head back to the north and keep on swimming in that direction. It changed course and began swimming straight towards me. I was far too close. I hadn't expected this!

What should I do? My mind raced.

I have to stay out of its way, I remembered. I stopped swimming and tried to back off. The shark kept coming towards me. There were no other swimmers nearby. I had deliberately stayed on my own. The faster swimmers were on the other side of the fish and I couldn't see them.

Was I in trouble? I didn't know. Whale sharks are supposed to be gentle creatures. What if this one wasn't?

They are filter feeders, but I knew they sometimes take a huge gulp of sea water. What if it did that, and that gulp included me? My heart began to pound.

I didn't want to turn my back on it but I did. I turned and swam away as fast as I could because the whale shark continued its turn. It was now swimming back the way it had come. I was in the path of a young adult fish that weighed over nine tonnes. I had to get out of its way — fast. The expedition leaders hadn't mentioned anything about them turning south.

After it passed me, that giant fish let fly with a burst of faeces. I tried to swim away from the brown scum. A ten-metre fish can hold an enormous amount of excrement! Had my presence scared it? There was no mention in the glossy brochures of this happening. Was it a defence mechanism?

The whale shark turned north again after swimming south for a couple of hundred metres. Once back on course, it dived. And all those pesky humans around it were no longer a bother.

That was it; that was the end of my whale shark adventure. As the adrenalin rush subsided, I swam back towards the boat where our team leader was already waiting to take my fins off for me and make sure the oldest member of her team climbed aboard safely.

Then the youngest member of the team, Essie, was there. Karen, the team leader, deftly lifted the four-year-old onto the boarding platform. All the others were back soon and waiting to board.

"I've never seen anything like that happen before," said Karen to the group of tourists when we were all on board the expedition boat again. "Are you okay after that experience?" She looked at me.

"I think so," I answered, "but I wasn't sure if it was angry with me and going to attack."

"No. They don't attack people," she said. "They are very placid animals. I saw you back-paddling to keep out of its way. That's all you could have done."

This was the biggest and last of the four whale sharks we swam with that day. It had been an unforgettable day. I'll never forget my panic as it turned and swam directly towards me but the worst part was being covered in shark shit.

---

* This story was first published in *HPA Magazine,* issue 4 2019.

First Impressions

Linda Visman

Charmaine wasn't nearly as pretty as her name. With dark hair and features, she was stocky in build, and her clothes looked like they came from the cheapest racks of the op shop. It was hard to tell her age. Maybe forty, I thought, seeing a few strands of grey hair. She'd suddenly stopped at my front fence.

"Am I going the right way to the shops?"

She sounded tentative. I looked up at her and smiled. I understood being shy.

"Yes, you are. Turn left at the crossroads. The shops are right there."

"Thanks. I've just moved here and wasn't sure of the way."

She smiled and her whole appearance was transformed. Her smile lit up her eyes and brightened her slightly lop-sided features, making them interesting instead of unattractive. She looked at my son, riding his trike on the driveway.

"How old is your boy? He looks about the same age as my daughter."

"Geoff's four – my youngest. The other two are at school."

We chatted for several minutes, exchanging family details. She had two sons and a daughter, and her family had just come to the city from Nyngan in Central West New South Wales. As she left, I threw out the invitation.

"It's hard being in a new place when you don't know anyone. Come any time. Maybe the kids can play together."

"Yes, perhaps." Her smile was uncertain.

My friend, Anne, was appalled when I told her about Charmaine, especially when I said I'd invited her to visit.

"You're joking! She's an Abo. They're troublemakers. Her kids must be the new ones at the school. I've heard they're a problem."

I asked my kids about them when they came home from school. Eleven-year-old Ian was casual.

"Yeah, Kyle's in my class. He doesn't do anything much except draw pictures — he's good at that. Him and his little brother stick together at recess."

"Yeah, Damon's in my class", eight-year-old Paul added. "There's a little sister too, but she doesn't come to school."

In the next weeks, I saw Charmaine walk past a few times, but she never called in. I supposed she was too shy or too busy. I knew they were still around at least, as Paul mentioned how Kyle and Damon were still not joining in. I told my boys they could help by being friendly towards them.

"I like Kyle. His pictures are great — 'specially the animals. He seems sad though."

"Yeah, Damon's real good at drawing too."

I wondered why those two lads were so quiet. Was something wrong at home? Did Charmaine need support? I didn't really want to get involved if there was trouble.

My husband said I shouldn't prejudge people. He suggested I take our youngest for a walk by Charmaine's place. I'd learned where she lived, so it was just a matter of getting up the courage. Maybe she'd appreciate some company, and her daughter could play with Geoff. When Paul told me the boys hadn't been at school all week. I decided to go the next day.

As we approached Charmaine's house, I could see several cars parked outside. Charmaine and two boys were at the front door. I couldn't see her daughter. A dark-haired man stood on the grass – her husband? Other adults stood around the front yard, and a dozen kids of all ages and shades of brown played among them.

Looks like she has plenty of people after all, I thought. *I should have known an Aboriginal family wouldn't be left alone. I needn't have worried about her.*

I felt like an intruder. I had just decided to turn back, when Charmaine looked across and saw me. She waved and headed to the gate to meet me, a smile on her face.

"Hello."

"Hi, Charmaine. I thought I'd call by and see how you've settled in, but it looks like you have company."

"That's all right. I haven't had time to drop in, but I wanted to say thank you."

"What for?" I was puzzled.

"Your boys have been real nice to Kyle and Damon at school. It's been good to have someone stick up for them and not call them names like the others. They've had a hard time lately."

I was amazed. I hadn't realised her boys were being harassed – or that mine had defended them. Charmaine went on.

"I'd really like it if you could join us. You can meet my husband, Jimmy. We're about to have a celebration of our daughter's life."

"Your daughter's – life?"

"Yes, didn't you know? Chantelle had advanced leukemia. That's why we came here – for the hospital. She passed away last Saturday while we were all with her. We've just come back from the funeral, and now we're having a get-together to give thanks for our wonderful little girl."

---

* This story was awarded third prize in the Writer's Friend Literary Competition, 2009.

Geiki Gorge

Margaret Young

At Geiki Gorge,
we boarded flat-bottomed boats
breaking reflections
from the rocks.

We heard water slurp
and slough as it slapped their sides,
watched them become darker
when painted by water.

Bright spears of reflected light
zigzagged anywhere
finding small caves
and freshwater crocodiles.

We listened to stories of
Koori dreaming and,
absorbing their pride,
responded to nature's spirituality.

Mary

Elizabeth Hunt

Rachel trembled when she heard the noise, but this time it was different. Instead of one loud bang, there was a regular creaking.

She was in the house alone. Ted had gone to a conference in Melbourne and wouldn't be back until the next day. Not that he ever heard any strange sounds at night. She had to shake him vigorously to waken him.

Rachel didn't want to go and investigate on her own. She'd never believed in ghosts, but now she had her doubts. How could any person get inside when everything was locked? She snuggled further down into the bed. After all, it had only happened twice before, she reasoned, and she and Ted had found no one, although they'd searched every room both times. Also, the noise soon stopped. Always before she'd managed to wake Ted. No wonder he thought she'd dreamt the whole thing.

She rolled onto her side and hoped to go back to sleep. But she couldn't. She waited, listening for the sobbing to start, as it had done last time. But only the creaking continued. After a couple of minutes, she could stand it no longer. She picked up the large torch on the bedside table and left her bed.

Bare-footed, Rachel padded along the upstairs passageway in the dark. The four bedrooms and two bathrooms were shrouded in a sombre stillness. With a firm hand on the banister, Rachel avoided stepping on any squeaking floorboards, as she descended the wooden staircase.

Once she reached the ground floor, she stood stock-still, listening. The creaking was close. She ignored the front rooms, and despite her pounding heart, crept towards the dining room. The noise grew louder. After taking a deep breath, she opened the door. She shivered as a cold blast of air swept across her. *Sometimes one has to face up to danger.* She flicked on the light. The room seemed empty.

Rachel was relieved to see everything in its place and she was the only person there. The casement window was moving back and forth in the wind, sounding like an ungreased playground swing. *I mustn't have closed that properly.*

She walked down the hall to the kitchen and was enjoying a cup of cocoa when the bang came. She froze.

She heard a girl's voice.

"Oh, Mary, Mary!"

The sobbing followed.

Rachel looked around for somewhere to hide. She could go outside through the back door, but the intruders might be there. She tiptoed to the pantry and slipped inside. *I'm probably a sitting duck here, but I daren't turn the light off.*

It stayed silent, but Rachel remained in the little recess until daybreak.

Ted didn't say much the next day, when she told him about the incident. *He probably thinks I've been dreaming again.*

~

The following Saturday afternoon, Rachel was weeding in the front garden, when she heard voices from the street. She looked up. An elderly couple were standing on the footpath gazing at her house. She walked across the lawn to them.

"Can I help you?" she asked.

The tall man smiled. "We were admiring your house. My wife used to live here, didn't you, Enid?"

The stout woman nodded and moved forward to steady herself against the fence.

"Really?" said Rachel.

She waited for a reply. When none was forthcoming, Rachel introduced herself and explained that she and her husband had moved to the town in the last few months.

The man, Bill, told her that they were staying for the weekend to have a look around.

Enid remained silent.

"Did you live here with your family?" Rachel asked.

"No. Although it was a long time ago."

"Go on, Enid," Bill urged.

"This was a boarding house, and I stayed here when I was a typist at the Bank of New South Wales." She paused. "The old place doesn't look to have changed after all those years. At least on the outside."

"That's right. Actually, it's only the kitchen and bathrooms that have been altered. Would you like to have a look inside?"

"Oh, that would be wonderful, wouldn't it, Enid?" said Bill.

"Yes," she replied softly. "But we don't want to put you or your family out."

"You won't. There's only me at home. I'm one of those golf widows, you know."

As they passed through each room, the couple made complimentary remarks. But Enid's blue eyes sparkled when they entered one of the bedrooms.

"This was my room. I shared it with ... Jenny, I think. Or was her name Joan? Anyway, she was a real live wire. I wonder what happened to her?"

"You didn't keep in touch?" asked Rachel.

"No. She went to live overseas I think."

"This is a big house for two people," said Bill.

"Yes. But we have a large family who like to come and stay. Later, we might turn it into a B&B."

At the foot of the stairs, Rachel offered them a cup of tea.

"That's if you don't mind sitting in the kitchen. It's just that my clothes are grubby from the garden."

"Oh, that's very kind, but we don't want to trouble you any further. You've been marvellous showing us around," replied Enid.

"It's no bother. I'm going to have a cuppa, so you may as well join me."

As they sipped their tea, Rachel decided to throw caution to the winds. *It might be rather rude of me, but this is too good an opportunity to pass up.* "Enid," she asked, "Did anything strange happen in this house while you were here?"

"No. Why do you ask?"

"I've heard unusual noises and crying at night a couple of times."

Bill broke in. "You mean you think this house is haunted?"

"Possibly."

"I don't believe in ghosts," said Enid. "And no one mentioned anything like that when I was here. Maybe you heard animals outside. Cats often sound like small children."

Bill cleared his throat. "Something odd did happen."

Enid frowned at him. "What are you talking about?"

"Remember when Lottie from here visited some years ago, and you both talked about old times?"

"Of course. But I don't see what you're getting at."

"She spoke of a girl's disappearance. A maid I think."

Enid looked worried. "My memory's not so good these days."

"Well, I can remember the basics," said Bill. "The girl who disappeared was the niece of the landladies – three unmarried sisters. One night she went missing after she'd cleaned up from the evening meal. Her bed wasn't slept in and all her clothes were still in her room the next morning. There were rumours that she'd run off with some man, or been abducted."

"She's never been found?" Rachel asked.

"No," Bill continued. "Lottie assured us that nobody's seen neither hide nor hair of her since then. And that must be thirty-five years ago. Wasn't that around the time when you left here, Enid?"

"I'm not sure. I left because I got a transfer for work."

"Was this maid called Mary?" asked Rachel.

"No," said Enid. "Her name was ... Deirdre or Doris? No ... Dorothy, that was it."

"Why did you think she might have been called Mary?" asked Bill.

"I've heard a girl calling out 'Mary' some nights, and sobbing."

"That's awful for you!" exclaimed Bill.

"Dreadful," said Enid quietly.

Bill's face was serious. "Maybe something involving a Mary happened later. I wish we could help, but can't see how."

Rachel accompanied them to the gate.

"The bolt doesn't line up properly," she explained. "We must get it fixed."

As Enid stepped onto the footpath, a thin, grey-haired woman approached.

"Hello Rosemary," called Rachel.

"Oh, hello."

Rosemary, a nearby neighbour, intended to keep on walking, but Rachel stopped her to introduce Enid and Bill, and to explain their interest in the house.

"Do you remember this place when it was a boarding house, Rosemary?" Rachel asked.

"No. But then I've only been here a few years. The Fitzgeralds, the family you bought it from, lived here then."

She nodded to Enid and Bill. "Nice to meet you, but I really must go."

You don't strike me as a very sociable person, Rosemary, thought Rachel. *You always make some excuse when I ask you in for a cuppa.*

Enid continued to watch Rosemary.

"What is it?" asked Bill.

"Oh nothing," Enid replied.

"Do you think you know her?" he persisted.

"No. I don't know anyone called Rosemary. It's just that she reminds me of someone … Anyway, she's getting around well for someone about my age, certainly more sprightly than I am."

Bill put a hand on her shoulder. "You're doing all right dear. And anyway, she might be a lot younger than she looks."

They exchanged good-byes, with Enid and Bill promising to call again, next time they visited the town.

~

Six weeks later, Ted was demolishing a shed out the back, to make way for a rose garden.

"Some of these floorboards have been replaced," he remarked to Rachel when she came to see how he was progressing.

"White ants?" she suggested.

He shrugged.

Ted soon had the area cleared.

"Think we'll have to replace this compacted soil with fresh," he told her, "But I'll give it a bit of a dig."

"I doubt you'll make much headway with that fork. I'll bring you the pick."

Ten minutes later he called Rachel.

"What's wrong?" she asked. "You look washed out. Perhaps you'd better stop for a while and rest."

"I'll certainly be stopping. Come and tell me what you make of this."

"Oh no!"

"Oh, yes … they're human."

During the next few days, Rachel called on her neighbours to offload her bumper lemon crop. When she told Rosemary her news about the body in the garden, the older woman turned pale and collapsed into a chair on the verandah.

"Oh, Rosemary, I didn't mean to upset you. Do you think you know who it is?"

"No. I just got a shock. It's such a horrible thing to have happened in our quiet little town. I'll be fine. Thank you so much for the lemons."

The following week, Rachel saw her at the library, returning books.

"Are you all right Rosemary?" she asked. "You don't look well."

"I'm just tired and worried. I've been packing to leave next week. My sister's very ill, and as she's only got me, I must go and look after her. Fortunately, I have only been renting here, so it's easy to move."

"Are you not coming back?"

"I don't know. Certainly not for some time, because Beatrice has a slowly progressive illness."

"I'm so very sorry."

"Thanks."

Rachel insisted that she drive Rosemary home.

~

Two months after Ted's grim discovery, Rachel met the postman at her gate.

"Any more excitement here?" he asked.

"No. We planted a special rose for her, above where we found the bones. It's called the Mary Rose."

"That's nice." He handed her two letters.

"Thanks. But can't you bring me something nicer than bills?"

"What about the other? It looks personal."

She turned it over. He began to move away.

"Stop!" she called after him. "This isn't mine."

"Sorry. Oh, Mary Smith." He smiled. "That'll be Rosemary Smith, who used to live three doors up."

"Are you sure?"

"Oh yes. It's happened a few times, and she'd always take them. I suppose some people shortened her name. Don't know where she's gone do you? She left no forwarding address."

An icy chill ran through Rachel. She had to swallow before she could answer.

"She said to her sister's, but they'd be moving, so no point in giving me any contact details."

"Well, we'll be keeping this for a while," he said, as he waved the letter. "So, if you do hear from her, you can let me know."

Rachel pursed her lips. *And pigs might fly.*

That afternoon she moved the Mary Rose to the far end of the bed and planted a Dorothy Perkins in its place.

Turning Point

Linda Visman

Sun gleams on her dark body
as she rises from the water
sweeps tangled hair back from her face.
She pushes through the waves
into the shallows, then turns
and gazes back out to sea.

A girl of perhaps twelve summers,
she wears a necklace of gleaming shells
strung onto a cord made from her own hair.
This and a belt also woven from her hair
are all that she wears.

She absently licks salt water from full lips.
Waves swirl the sand around her feet
but she takes no notice of them.
Seawater trickles down her back
and strong brown legs.

Dark brown eyes, heavy-lashed and pensive
are fixed upon the endless waves.
Rollers break upon nearby rocks,
but she seems oblivious to their roar,
though she is well aware
of the powerful spirits
that inhabit those churning waters.

Of what does this slender
newly-made young woman dream?
Does she see a young, virile and
handsome lover in the ocean depths?
Or does she simply regret
the loss of her childhood?

At a gruff call, she sighs.
Turning from the pounding surf,
she walks across the sand.
A lean and grizzled old warrior
waits for her at the top of the sand-hill.
Earlier today, she became
his third and junior wife.

---

* This poem was published in *HPA Magazine,* issue 2 2019.

The End of the Line

Jan Mitchell

Garry stepped down from the carriage. He shaded his eyes against the sun, which shone low in the clear blue sky. He looked around to check whether anyone was watching him. Seeing no one, he shouldered his backpack and sauntered off to his quiet spot. Whenever he returned from the noise of the city and the train journey, unless it was raining, Garry sat in isolation on this particular tree stump. He closed his eyes and, after inhaling the dry scent of the surrounding eucalyptus and wattle, he began to meditate. It was one of the few secrets he didn't share with Nina, his wife. He knew she missed him when he was away all day, and that she would feel hurt that he didn't want to rush home to her.

Half an hour later, he heard the next train from the city slow as it approached. Daylight was fading. Feeling calm and completely centred, Garry rose and made his way to the platform so that he would appear to be alighting from this later train.

~

Nina drove down the road past the tip to the local railway station. The sun was sinking behind the hills, tingeing them a deep red. She turned on the headlights. Radio National was on and her interest was piqued by Damien Carrick's words. He was interviewing an ex-criminal, Tony Michaels, on a pre-recorded episode of *The Law Report.*

"You say prison is so dehumanising these days that you don't become rehabilitated — you just become dehumanised."

"That's right," said Tony Michaels, "You'll do anything at all to take your anger out on the rest of society — on the bastards who were complicit in your torture. 'Cos that's what it was — torture."

"Could you tell us a bit more about that torture?"

"They try to eliminate your identity. You're dressed the same, you eat the same, the cells are the same. You can't choose anything. You've even got to shit when they say you can."

Nina thought he had a point. She couldn't handle prison at all — too claustrophobic. But this Tony had obviously done something terrible and it was right he should be punished for it.

"Many people would say that is a fitting punishment for the crime for which you've been convicted. How would you answer them?"

"I'd accept that to a certain extent, but Jeez man, you can't even choose your cell mate. The bastard I shared with snored all night. In my book, that's torture. That's every night for six months. Then they rotate you to another prison after six months. I thought I might get a better cell mate, but nah. The next one sleep-walked every night and tried to get into my bed. I'm supposed to be working in the laundry next day. I'm so tired I scald myself."

"If you're put into a work program, doesn't that give you some self-esteem — you know — a job well done, that sort of thing?"

"Ha ha ha. Those are shit jobs. There's no self-esteem there — it's slave labour. As for the guards, they're just bullies. That's the sort of fella goes into a job like that. Gotta think themselves tough."

"Do you feel you received any kind of rehabilitation?"

"Nah."

Nina drove into the tiny, deserted station carpark. She tilted her seat back, relaxing with closed eyes while she waited for the train from the city to deliver her husband home.

~

Garry climbed the steps to the overpass. Looking down, he could see their Ford parked there. Nina was waiting, as he knew she would be.

He approached the car and saw the shattered windscreen. He peered through the hole, then opened the driver's door.

"Nina," he cried to her slumped body, "What's happened? Are you okay?"

Garry pushed Nina's shoulder back and took in the smell of fresh blood. The front of her head was crushed. There was wet blood on her face. Her mouth was twisted, silently screaming. Her eyes stared vacantly.

He dug into his left-hand pocket for his mobile phone. Fumbling with shock, his bloodied fingers finally managed to press the buttons. But there was no reception. He ran back up the overpass. At the top there was just enough reception for his call to go through.

"Ambulance and police – station carpark – urgent – head injury – unconscious."

Once he'd made the emergency call, shock began to set in. Garry stumbled back down the steps and collapsed next to the car, his forehead in his hands. He was shaking. It was beyond his comprehension. Who could have done this to his beloved wife? Why? The bastard couldn't be far away.

~

A police car arrived first. Two constables climbed out, a man and a woman. They took in the partially lit scene. An older man was slumped on the gravel, head in his hands, a backpack still on his shoulders. The car, five or six years old, was neatly parked and had a head-sized hole in the windscreen.

Pulling on a pair of surgical gloves, the male policeman approached the car, leaned in and turned off the radio. He placed his gloved fingers on the driver's neck to feel for a pulse. He shook his head.

His colleague stood beside Garry. "Excuse me, sir, I'm Constable Bluett. Did you call emergency services?"

"Nina, my wife, is … how badly is she hurt? … She's unconscious … I didn't want to touch anything … Who would do this to her?" Garry stood up unsteadily. "Where's the ambulance? She needs medical help, now!"

The policewoman eyed Garry carefully, taking in his state of dress, demeanour and the drying blood on his hands and face.

The male constable came over. He, too, noticed the blood.

"Sir, I'm Constable Klein. Your name, please."

Garry stared at him blankly. "Wha… What did you say?"

"I asked you your name, sir."

"Oh. Ga… Garry." He was shaking. Was this a nightmare?

"Garry. Do you have another name, Garry?"

"Nesbitt."

"And the lady in the car? What is her name?"

"My wife? She needs an ambulance."

"Just answer the question."

"Name's Nina Nesbitt."

"Okay. Now, tell me what's happened here."

"I dunno. Got off the train as usual. Nina was waiting for me, but this ...?"

A second car arrived and the constable sauntered over to it and spoke at the open window. A detective climbed out and crossed to Garry.

"Good evening sir. I'm Senior Detective Thomas. I believe you are Garry Nesbitt. Is that correct?"

Garry nodded.

"Who owns this vehicle? Who's the registered owner?"

"Me. It's registered in my name."

"How old are you, Garry?"

"I'm sixty-seven."

Thomas nodded to Constable Klein who went to his car to check the registration details.

"Where do you live?" Thomas continued his questions.

"Tw...Twenty-five, The Es...Esplanade, Minington."

"And where have you been today?"

"Sydney."

"What were you doing in Sydney?"

"A specialist's appointment."

"Where was that?"

"Royal North Shore. The Specialist Centre there."

"What kind of specialist?"

"Ah..."

"Answer the question please."

"Psychiatrist." The detective continued writing notes in his notebook.

"Okay. Now what time did you arrive at the station here?"

"What's going on? Where's the ambulance? I need to go to the hospital with my wife, with Nina."

"Just answer my question. What time did you arrive here at the station?"

"Fi... I came in on the five-thirty Sydney to Newcastle train. I rang Nina when I was about to catch the train at Hornsby — told her what time I'd be back."

"What did she say to you?"

"Said, 'I'll pick you up'."

"Did she say anything else?"

"Asked if I'd had a good day."

"Had you had a good day? Did anything make you angry while you were in Sydney or on the train? Did you argue with your wife last night, or this morning, before you caught the train?"

"No. Of course not!"

Thomas moved off to confer with his colleague. Garry strained to hear their conversation.

"... usually the husband ... blood on his face. Take him in."

Garry stumbled towards the car and thumped the bonnet.

"Where's the fucking ambulance? It should be here by now. Nina needs help. She needs a hospital."

"The ambulance is on its way. We are doing all we can to help."

Just then, the ambulance pulled into the car park and the paramedics opened the back door from where they removed a stretcher.

"Come with me, please sir," said Detective Thomas. "We'll continue our enquiries at the station. The ambulance is here now. There's nothing more we can do here."

"No ... Nooo! I can't leave Nina." Garry emitted a long keening wail. "Nooooooo.... She's unconscious. I need to be with her when she comes round. Some lowlife has hit her over the head. When I looked, she was still bleeding. You should be searching for the culprit."

"We'll keep you informed about your wife's condition. If you wish, you can call a solicitor from the station."

Garry shook his head. It had to be a nightmare. He shook his head a second time, but the flashing lights of the police cars and the ambulance were still there, brilliant in the darkness.

Before he climbed into the police car, he turned and shouted over his shoulder to the paramedics, "Be gentle with her. She's hurt. She's hurt real bad."

Garry slumped forward in the back seat beside the other detective and sobbed.

~

Tony held his breath as he watched from the bushes. He saw one police car leave with the man who'd got off the train at five o'clock. He knew he'd have to go soon. But he couldn't draw himself away — not yet. His adrenalin was pumping hard. He still clenched the lump of concrete between the now bloodless fingers of his right hand.

The ambos pulled the woman out of the driver's seat. They placed her on a stretcher, covered it and put it into the back of the ambulance.

The constables were securing the car and putting up crime scene tape.

Tony knew he had to go now. Steadying his breathing, he walked south down the access track alongside the line. About two hundred metres on he threw the concrete as far into the bushes as he could and then, where the fence stopped, he crossed the tracks. The police didn't notice him in his black clothes and balaclava. As he climbed the embankment on the far side, he could just make out the remaining police tying off the crime scene tape around the damaged car.

He pulled off his balaclava, and returned to the station, remaining wherever possible in the shadows. When a northbound train pulled in, Tony came out from behind the covered area and climbed into the middle carriage. He stayed in the vestibule until the train reached the next station. There he alighted and crossed on the overpass to the other side of the station. He walked calmly as far as he could to the top end of the platform. Tony waited there for the six-forty express to Sydney.

A couple of days later, Tony saw the news item. There had been a court hearing in Toronto and the police had remanded in custody Garry Nesbitt, sixty-seven, of Minington, in relation to the murder of his wife, Nina Nesbitt.

Tony's mouth twitched into a slight grin. He pulled out his map of New South Wales and closing his eyes, he stabbed his finger at the map.

"Bathurst next," he whispered.

His eyes gleamed.

---

* An earlier version of this story (under the title 'Tony was Angry') was selected for commendation in the Alice Sinclair Memorial Writing Competition in 2018.

Out of the Rapids

Alison Ferguson

I waited my turn to clamber out of the minibus. I'd learned years ago that being last brought opportunities. Backpacks sat behind their owners, after all. You'd be amazed how slack people are about where they put their money. Ruby's mobile was sticking out from her pocket, just begging for escape but our science teacher, Mr Napier, stuck his long nose in, telling us to get a move on. I couldn't see why. The river wasn't going anywhere. I was in no hurry to develop *team bonding,* as old Napier kept telling us. He's the Deputy Principal, so I figure he's got to try to sell that sort of crap, but I don't see why I should buy it.

The other students set about earning brownie points by helping him and Miss Easterbrook pull down the canoes. It was cold outside the fug of the bus, so I wandered about the clearing and stared at the battered Council sign with faded pictures of all the biting ants, poisonous spiders, snakes and rash-inducing vegetation that we'd find in the river gorge. In the midday quiet of the bush, the only sounds were the rustle of leaves in the tree tops and the leisurely burble of the river. When they'd said *rapids,* I'd expected something a bit louder.

A guy in Steve Irwin khakis beckoned us over and read the riot act about no skylarking, no smoking, yada yada. I wasn't paying much attention until Max piped up. You can usually rely on Max to put teachers on the spot.

"So, is there any way out of the gorge between here and where we finish?" he asked, flashing me a quick look.

From the texts he'd been sending me the whole way here, it sounded like he was a man with a plan. I'd played dumb, but if it got me out of this stupid excursion then I was up for it.

Steve Irwin nodded, "Good question. The first set of rapids is pretty easy, the second set is the hardest, and the third is a piece of cake. So, if you're not coping on the first, then watch out for the ramp on your left, straight after you're through. You can pull in and then make your way up the track to the top of the cliff. Mind you, you'll be carrying the canoe."

Everyone groaned.

"And the other exit?" asked Ruby.

Given the eyes she was making at Max, it looked like he wasn't the only one looking for better things to be doing than paddling. I was going to have to move fast to make sure I got to go in Max's canoe.

"There is an exit that comes up on your right, straight after the second set. As I said earlier, the second set is the most difficult, particularly after all the rain we had last week," Steve Irwin said with a grim chuckle.

That didn't sound good to me. I'm too skinny to be any good at sports and stuff. I don't mind coming and watching on sports day, even though Max thinks it's next level cringe. The number of bags dumped in the change rooms makes for a good haul. You have to be quick — a lot of parents come to that sort of thing and, even though they usually have eyes only for their little darlings, you can never predict when they're going to start fussing about. And if Miss Easterbrook's on duty then forget it. The woman's got eyes in the back of her head.

Steve Irwin was rabbiting on. "So, if you're still with your canoe, which I hope you will be if you've been listening, then stay on the river. But if you've lost the canoe, head to the rock ledge in amongst the reeds. I wouldn't recommend it unless you have to. The ledge can be tricky to find, and it's a steep climb."

After those reassuring words there was silence.

Mr Napier started reading our names off his list, allocating us to our canoes.

"Sarah, you're with me," he finished.

Mr Napier gave me that look, you know the one that teachers give you when they think you're a complete waste of space. He'd been giving me that look every science lesson this year. I'd thought he was on to me a few days back but nothing happened. He probably thought he'd be able to keep a better eye on me if I was stuck in his canoe.

I looked over to Max, but the bastard just shrugged and began helping Ruby to stow her gear at the back of their canoe. Ruby's smile at me was pure saccharine as they paddled off together.

Mr Napier and I were the last to leave. He took the back end of the canoe. I could feel his eyes boring holes between my shoulder blades. I started to paddle as fast as I could — the quicker we made it to the end, the happier I'd be.

"Easy does it, Sarah," he puffed. "Let the river do the work."

I slowed down, not because he said to, but my arms were beginning to ache and we hadn't even got to the first rapid. The trees closed in around us as the river narrowed. I could only see up to the escarpment. It felt like no-one but us had ever been there. The river got noisier and from the bush rose the noise of a million birds and insects. I could see more turbulence ahead, and the white caps were higher, but there were only two big boulders, and the way through to the calmer water ahead seemed fairly obvious. I spotted the concreted ramp that Steve Irwin had mentioned.

I paddled like fury and we skimmed by the boulders. By the time we were coming out of the rapids our canoe must have been going ninety klicks. As we flashed past, I caught sight of Max and Ruby dragging their canoe up the ramp.

It was all a bit of an anti-climax. Not that I'd tell anyone, of course, but I'd been a bit worried about the whole rapids-thing.

"Well done, Sarah."

If Mr Napier was shooting for charm, then it was a bit late after four years of giving me a hard time.

"So, Sarah," he said, wheezing with the effort of talking and paddling. "I wanted to have a word with you about a worrying report I received —"

He stopped talking and I didn't know if I was meant to say something. My heart went into overdrive. It thumped away as if we were canoeing down the Niagara Falls, not meandering along on this flat stretch. Shit and fuckin' shit. Just say nothing.

"Stay sharp, Sarah." His voice was stretched taut with tension.

The river came back into focus but too late. Within seconds our canoe began to tip. I looked back to Mr Napier. He was ploughing his paddle deep into the water, trying to slow us down against the current. His face was frozen, eyes fixed at the water beyond me. Then, caught in the swirling water, the canoe rolled. For a moment, as I emerged from the fast-flowing water, I thought I was safe. Then I was wrenched into a tumbling, churning spin-cycle. Seconds, minutes, hours later, I emerged, one hand clawed around the paddle.

Ahead, I saw Mr Napier's bald head bobbing intermittently into view. I tried to swim towards him but I didn't want to lose my paddle. The river was bent on taking me to the opposite bank and into the base of a sheer cliff. Each time I came up for air, the cliff was closer. With a last attempt, I used my paddle to propel away from the rocks. I shot into a turbulent cascade down between the boulders.

At its base, the thunderous water thrust me deep and held me there, where green turned to grey and swirls of dirt and pebbles scoured my cheeks. My paddle was gone. My lungs were bursting. My ribs screamed for breath but the press of water pinned me down. I was going to die, for all that it mattered. It wasn't as if anyone would miss me — not Mum, certainly not Dad, not Max. No-one is allowed to say bad things about the dead. It wouldn't matter what I'd done. I hung, suspended in the weight of water above, waiting. Mr Napier would have to find someone else to pick on.

Something knocked against the top of my head. A paddle? I reached up and made a grab for it and, the moment I had a hold, it tugged away as if tempting me to rise. My shoes scraped against the loose gravel of the river floor. I pushed off, chasing that damn paddle, up to the light, air knifing into my lungs.

"Over here, there's a ledge."

Mr Napier?

All I could see were reeds. I thrashed about, trying to find a way through.

The end of the paddle poked out of the reeds.

"Grab it. I'll pull you in," he rasped.

He dragged me up and onto the rocky ledge. I lay flat on my back, sucking in breath after breath, savouring each one.

"Are you all right? Is anything broken?"

"I'm fine." I waved him away.

Cautiously I sat up, my body aching with each movement. I shivered as the sun disappeared and the light around us lost its colours.

"What about the others?" I asked.

"I think they must all have got through. Miss Easterbrook will take them straight back to the school. Their parents will be worried if they're late returning. She'll let your mother know what's happened, I'm sure."

I snorted. Catching Mr Napier's look of surprise, I added, "But they'll call the police, or rescue people, won't they? As long as we stay put, they'll find us."

He shook his head. "It's too exposed near the river. We won't be able to get all the way up to the escarpment tonight, but it should be warmer away from the river. No, we'll follow the emergency plan, as arranged."

I got to my feet, gingerly testing my weight. As far as I could tell, no bones were broken. My water bottle, hooked to my utility belt, had also survived. I felt in my inside pocket, where the sandwich I'd made this morning was a sodden glad-wrapped mass.

Within the first few steps the shadows increased. The constant spray and mist rising from the river made the ground underfoot slippery with moss. My drenched sandshoes squelched. I couldn't feel my toes.

Higher up, the ground became drier. It was still so steep that I had to grab hold of the straggly ferns on either side to help myself up. Mr Napier was silent and his longer legs increased the distance between us. My wet clothes chafed. Every few steps, I walked into clouds of tiny insects and had to cough and spit my mouth clear.

Finally, I couldn't see the path in front of me. I stopped and sat down, not caring whether I caught up with Mr Napier or not. The night air wrapped around me. I unclipped the water bottle and took a large gulp.

"Better be careful with that water." Mr Napier had come back. "That's all you've got."

I stoppered the bottle and clipped it back on my belt.

"There's a landing of sorts up ahead. We'll stop there for the night." He disappeared into the gloom.

When I reached him, I nearly tripped over his legs. He was sitting with his back propped against a tree. I sat cross-legged a short distance away. Looking at Mr Napier's tree, it struck me that ants at the base of it were a real possibility. I didn't feel like warning him.

Mr Napier stayed silent. I listened to the chirruping crickets till they settled into a lulling hum and then curled on my side, arm crooked under my head. I had almost managed to detach myself from the cold and was almost asleep when Mr Napier cleared his throat.

"As I was saying earlier, I should let you know that I've received a worrying report on your behaviour — things have been going missing."

I could only make out his outline dimly. His face was obscured in darkness. He was still sitting against the tree.

"As the Deputy Principal," he went on, "it's up to me to decide if the police should be involved."

I couldn't think of what to say. The cold I'd felt moments before was nothing compared to the ice spreading through me now.

"Do you have anything to tell me that might shed some light on this?" he asked.

"No." I was glad it was dark enough to hide my face.

The silence strung out like a bridge between us. I couldn't stand it.

"Look. I only went into to the change rooms to go to the loo, all right?" I blurted.

He waited.

A grinding weight fell into my stomach as I realised my mistake.

"The things went missing from the change rooms, Sarah." His voice was so soft that I had to strain to hear it.

"It wasn't me." I tried to keep my voice steady.

"You were seen."

The memory flooded in from weeks before — the look that Miss Easterbrook had given me as I came out of the change rooms.

"What will your parents say, Sarah?"

"Nothing."

Mr Napier sighed. "Look, I know that at your age, it can seem that everyone is against you, but parents really do care —"

"No, they don't," I shouted into the dark, sitting up now.

"Sarah, I'm just trying to understand," he said, his voice still soft. "Remember the science we covered about the river? You need four factors, acting by themselves or together, to make a rapid: gradient, constriction, obstruction and flow rate. It's tough changing the first three because they're locked into the landscape, unless you can change where you are. But flow rate can change. You're clearly hitting a rocky patch, but I need you to tell me about it, so I can see what can help steer you into calmer waters."

I was cold all the way through and his words just washed over me. I didn't care what he thought of me, what anyone thought.

"You lot think you know everything. Well, some parents don't care."

I was finished but, in the darkness, I could feel Mr Napier waiting, listening.

"My Dad didn't care when he left us. And Mum —" My voice broke. Why should I have to say it? To say it, made it real.

Still the darkness waited.

"And your mother ...," prompted Mr Napier.

"Mum only cares about one thing — when her dole cheque comes in so she can stock up her grog," I said, trying to keep my mind blank as I betrayed her. "Food doesn't grow on trees, you know," I finished lamely.

Mr Napier started to fidget. I could hear him scratching at his ankles.

"So, that's why —?"

Before he could finish, he leapt to his feet, brushing his clothes down and swearing. "Bloody ants." He stamped about, slapping at his clothes.

After a while, the rustling and stamping stopped. There was a shuffle in the dirt and I realised that he had moved to sit beside me on the ground. I sensed that he was looking at me directly.

"Thank you for telling me, Sarah. It helps us to know these things. When we understand, then we can help."

I was shaking uncontrollably, but it wasn't with cold. The tears were warm on my cheek, as warm as the sense of Mr Napier beside me.

"Bad luck about the ants," I said, wiping my face on my damp sleeve.

I felt him shrug.

The night felt strangely warm, as I waited for the dawn, listening to Mr Napier's breathing, knowing that he was awake with me as the stream widened out ahead.

Cut Thy Youth in Twain

KJ Mair

Juliet is obsessed with the thought of Romeo.

She likes the name Romeo. She likes how it tastes in her mouth, like ice cream at the first lick. The name sits at the tip of her tongue ready to roll forth at a moment's notice. It feels like it belongs on her gums and between her teeth.

Nobody understands.

How could they? No one knows Romeo like Juliet.

Juliet plunges the needle deep into the meaty part of her thigh and leans back into the chair in relief. If she squeezes her eyes tight enough, she can feel the whorls of Romeo's fingertips against her skin. And if she pitches her hum low enough she can hear the timbre of his deep voice vibrating in her ears.

It feels more right to her than the sun.

If only someone would try to understand.

Juliet's parents certainly don't.

They think it's just a phase. Sometime soon they believe she will stop talking about it. But the longer she talks and the longer she refuses to show any sign of letting go, the angrier they get.

Juliet's mother, Mrs Capulet plays with her pearls and sometimes she grips them so tightly, each little ball presses into her throat. Juliet is surprised that she's still breathing. Juliet cannot understand how a mother, feeling so stifled in her own life, would want to force that same kind of life on her child.

"Why aren't you like others girls, Juliet?" She's fiddling with her pearls again. "Why don't you at least meet with Paris? One date and you might forget all these silly notions of yours. You will give him a call, won't you young lady?" She sounds strangled.

There is a monster called Doubt that lives inside everyone. It eats away confidence and aims for the knees at every chance it gets. With every word her mother utters, Juliet can feel the monster grow inside her, until she feels her every thought is marked out with a big red *MISTAKE!*

Mrs Capulet puts her hand on her daughter's shoulder and squeezes. "Let's forget all about this Romeo business. Hmmm?"

Juliet closes her eyes and wishes to be anywhere but here. Romeo seems to be impossible to reach inside the high ornate walls of a place called home.

~

Nurse helps. She always does.

She's the one who slips Juliet the needles and the clothes and the chance of escape. Nurse lets her see Romeo. And how could Juliet not love her for that?

When Nurse rests a hand on her shoulder, Juliet feels warmth that is clearly absent from her mother's touch. She feels both glad and sad. She knows if Nurse is ever discovered aiding her rebellion she would be punished, probably sacked.

The demon named Guilt twists its way around in Juliet's guts. *Good then. Let it play with Doubt and they can eat each other for all I care.* But then she looks into Nurse's kind and wrinkly face and feels Guilt's tender talons scrape.

"Won't you get in trouble?"

Nurse grins and smoothes her hands across Juliet's shoulders. "I've been in trouble more times than a zebra has spots."

"Stripes."

"Really?" Nurse blinks in muddlement. "Well, in any case it isn't the first time and it certainly won't be the last." She smiles and sniffs, "Now go on, and go find your happy days."

Juliet surprises herself and Nurse as she hugs her hard. She feels something tight in her chest. For the first time she can't put a name to the feeling. Maybe it's not a demon after all.

Juliet backs away and tries to discreetly rub the tears off her cheeks. From the corner of her eye she can see Nurse doing the same. Roughly, she snatches up her backpack and slings it over her shoulder. With one final nod to Nurse she slips out of the room and outside to the balcony.

From there it is easy to climb down. Even with the rain and the slick, it's so damn easy. From between a gap in the clouds a full, envious moon lightens the night's sky with two stars that outshine the rest.

Juliet finally goes to find Romeo.

~

Juliet had picked the sharpest scissors she could find. The ones that cut cleanly from the first snip. At first she hesitates, because this is like death, isn't it?

Yes, says the monster called Doubt. *It is, and where would you be then? You know what, just a confused and sick little girl.*

Juliet drops the scissors and they clatter in the sink. She presses her hands deep into her eye sockets and just wants to scream.

Breathing in deeply, she squashes downs the monster and finally looks into the cracked mirror.

She doesn't like what she sees.

She never has.

She has always felt uncomfortable in her own skin and body. The hormone injections have helped. Doing what she's about to do is her first major step in changing her appearance and her life.

But isn't losing something just the first step in transformation? She picks up the scissors and commits, not to change, but to bare the real person beneath.

The hair cuts nicely, still wet from being assaulted by the storm as she had raced along the slippery pavement, looking for any sort of haven, a service station bathroom or a public toilet or anything. Anything. She had fallen, and scraped her hands and bloodied one knee. It was like growing pains.

Cutting her hair feels cleansing and shocking all at once. Locks litter the sink and plug up the drain. Juliet doesn't care, she feels freer and happier than she ever has. It feels like escaping a too tight skin or pulling out of a crusted cocoon.

When she's finished, she lays down the scissors and drums her fingers on the countertop. Nervous, but not afraid. Not doubtful. Not anymore.

She looks up.

Juliet smiles into the mirror and finally, finally Romeo he … *he* smiles back.

---

* This story was a finalist and selected for special mention in the *Newcastle Herald* Short Story Competition in 2016.

Contributors

All contributors are members the Lake Macquarie Branch of the Fellowship of Australian Writers (NSW) – abbreviated as LakeMacFAW in the following snapshots of what lies beneath the surface of their writing.

Alison Ferguson — Alison is one of the editors of this anthology. In her twenties, she completed a degree in writing but ended up getting a real job instead. Alison has been a member of LakeMacFAW since her retirement five years ago, aiming to get her creative writing to publication standards. She was thrilled to have a story shortlisted for the 2018 Scarlet Stiletto Awards, and to receive 1st Prize in the Margaret Cech Short Story Award in 2019. *Beneath the surface,* Alison may be an adrenalin-junkie; she once ended up shooting rapids in an isolated river in Papua New Guinea — entirely by accident. But no, she wouldn't do it again. (See www.backstorypress.com.)

Pam Garfoot — Pam is one of the editors of this anthology. She joined LakeMacFAW nearly six years ago, after she had already co-authored her first book, an award-winning family history entitled *Making them real*. Once in the writing group Pam spread her wings into other genres of writing — travel memoir, short stories, reviews and poems. Soon she hopes to publish her second co-authored book which is about Australian pioneer history. Beneath her calm and unruffled surface is a shy, nerdy person struggling to stay home and write.

Pam also enjoys painting in oils (portraits and landscapes), watercolour, and pen and ink illustration (which you can enjoy in this anthology). She currently paints in the studio of artist Margrete Erling (the Yara Balba Art Studio) at Mandalong, New South Wales. Her work has been exhibited locally: at Swansea Library as part of the Lake Macquarie Libraries' Launchpad program, in the Lake Macquarie Waste to Art Exhibition, and at the Tackshed Gallery in Mandalong. She has also received awards for her paintings at the Morisset Show.

George Graves — George has been a member of LakeMacFAW for about five years, writing short stories and some poems, mostly about people and relationships. Although they are largely fictional, he often draws on incidents from his past and incorporates these into the stories. George is proud of having his name amongst the authors of many professional papers during his working life. George owns an old yacht and enjoys messing about in it, where all the trivia of this world seems to fade away. He loves reading about many different topics, including mathematics and quantum physics. He shares his home at Lake Macquarie with a quirky, somewhat spoilt, ginger cat.

James Horn — James often wore a grey suit and tie in his former life as an accountant but more recently he set about writing stories of his mother's uncles and aunts and some of their descendants. A year ago, after deciding he needed some help, James joined LakeMacFAW. His stories cover 120 years of his family's involvement with British politics, war, industry, society, life in the 'colonies', and some sex thrown in. He feels that in any family there will be stories and gossip, coupled with actual facts beneath the surface. In another life James was a cattle farmer. Faced with a bull charging him on his horse, he dismounted and ran straight at the bull shouting very loudly. They all survived — but that's another story.

Elizabeth Horwitz — Elizabeth has had a love for the natural environment of Lake Macquarie since moving into the area over thirty years ago. For years, she has written poetry on this topic, amongst many others. Elizabeth is passionate about the arts. She is President of the Hunter Professional Arts organisation and edits its popular magazine. She has been a member of LakeMacFAW for ten years and acts as Public Officer for the group.

Elizabeth Hunt — Elizabeth began writing seven years ago, when she attended a memoir course at her local library. As well as describing aspects of her childhood, Elizabeth has ventured into fictional short stories and travel experiences. Throughout this period, Elizabeth has received help and encouragement from local writing courses and groups. These include the Lake Macquarie Library, the University of the Third

Age (U3A) and LakeMacFAW, whose critique sessions have provided valuable assistance. Now she's embarked on transforming her travel diaries into travel memoirs, which was her original reason for writing.

Sandra Joy — Sandra is a motivational and skilful writer with a strong personality. Having lost all her writings in four very different circumstances, she is now determined to share her life's research with her readers. Sandra has survived addictions and other traumas which she has overcome in a powerful way. Now, she is sharing those stories in her forthcoming book, *Salvation Through the Gift of Help,* to inspire people to rewrite their own life (due for publication 2020). We were pleased to welcome Sandra to LakeMacFAW this year.

Tony Lang — Tony has been a member of LakeMacFAW for approximately fifteen years. The first three of his five books are amusing accounts of his life as a parish minister in Australia and Scotland. He has also written three children's books. Tony's fifty years of ministry, including parish ministry, military, police and aged care chaplaincies provide a fine source of writing material into which he can delve. He is proud of his most recent book, *What the Bible Really Says About Women* which supports women's rights to leadership positions within the church and in the wider world. Tony's writing displays a love of all living creatures and a heightened awareness of the strange and mysterious. (See www.lachlanness.com.)

KJ Mair — Kristen (aka KJ Mair) is one of the editors of this anthology. She has been a keen writer for many years and a member of LakeMacFAW for the last eight. She has studied screenwriting at the Australian Film Television & Radio School and hopes to one day have her works published and seen on screen. She has won second prize in both the Alice Sinclair Memorial Prize and the *Newcastle Herald* Short Story Competition and has been a finalist on numerous occasions. Kristen is currently working on her first novel, a dark adult fantasy that deals with immortals and magical refugees living within the bones of an ancient dragon. She loves to make her fellow FAW members gasp in surprise with her twisted stories.

Jan Mitchell — New Zealander Jan Mitchell, a former English teacher, loves adventure and travel. For years, she published stories and photographs in sailing magazines. Now, she publishes her own books — stories about travel with her husband by yacht or campervan. These stories are illustrated by her own photographs. Occasionally, Jan also dabbles in fiction short stories. She joined LakeMacFAW in February 2007. (See www.writingsfromjanmitchell.com.)

Cate Plink – Cathrine (Cate) was born in New Zealand but has lived in Australia since 1969. She has been involved with the Fellowship of Australian Writers NSW since 1994 and is currently the Vice President and Competition Secretary of the State Committee (as well as an active member of LakeMacFAW). Cate likes writing short stories and has placed in a couple of competitions. She has also had her work in several small anthologies. Her passion, however, is for children's stories. Her first book, the novella *Mokes, Mines, and Mayhem,* was published in 2008, and she is currently working on a series of books for the middle school range.

Anita Richardson – Anita has been associated with LakeMacFAW for a number of years, and enjoys interacting with other writers. For some time, her main passion has revolved around the arts, with painting and photography being her particular interests. She also likes to spend time in nature and has a great love of beaches and the lake. In the past she could also be found sailing on the lake. Anita has added writing to her portfolio of artistic pursuits, and is proud to have been a finalist in the *Newcastle Herald* Short Story Competition. Being part of a writing group is something she finds inspiring and encouraging.

Rina Robinson — Rina was a founding member of LakeMacFAW from its inception over twenty years ago, and she continues to delight and inspire us with her subversive sense of humour and creativity. She received the Distinguished Service Award from the Fellowship of Australian Writers (NSW) in 2015. She enjoys writing short stories across genres, and her stories and poems have appeared in numerous anthologies. Rina was born in the UK and came to Australia after years of performing on stage and in cabaret. She is immensely proud of her Australian citizenship, as reflected in her writing which appeared in the anthology, *We are Australian: Australian Stories by Aussies* in 2010. In 2011, Rina published *Dawn of Darkness*, a Young Adult fantasy novella and, in 2013, she published *Views & Visions* which showcased her paintings as well as her poetry.

Linda Visman — Linda is one of the editors of this anthology. After the joys of wrangling snakes and kids in remote communities of the Northern Territory, Linda now lives a rather quieter life at Lake Macquarie. Since joining LakeMacFAW in 2005, Linda's creative writing has flowed into award-winning short stories, poetry and memoir pieces. In 2016, Linda received the Distinguished Service Award from the Fellowship of Australian Writers (NSW). In her blog, she writes on a variety of topics at www.wangiwriter.wordpress.com. Drawing on her early life experience, she has also published (so far) two Young Adult historical novels.

Margaret Young – Margaret has been a member of a number of branches of the Fellowship of Australian Writers for over fifty years and is currently a member of LakeMacFAW. Her stories reflect family remembrances as well as personal experiences. In 1998 she won the Henry Lawson Adult Short Story Competition winning not only prize money but a small statue of Henry Lawson. She believes, if able, in volunteering in organisations that help others. Through being a volunteer in the Voluntary Aid Detachment for the Red Cross, she was selected to work in Malaysia in 1967 and Vietnam in 1968. Margaret has had two poetry chapbooks published through Picaro Press. *From a Distance (2017)* reflects her love of nature and quirkiness, and *Round Eye in Vietnam* describes her experiences during and after the war.

———

www.ingramcontent.com/pod-product-compliance
Lightning Source LLC
Chambersburg PA
CBHW070637170726
48291CB00003B/1043

* 9 7 8 1 8 7 6 4 0 9 6 3 0 *